The Lig[illegible]le of Serious Croquet

David Appleton

Published in Great Britain by David Appleton,
Newcastle upon Tyne, 1996.

The cartoons and photographs, except for those on page 93 which were produced by means of Photo-CD™, were scanned using Ofoto™, the technical drawings were created with ClarisDraw™, the musical notation was realised by HB Music Engraver™, and the text was written in Pagemaker™. The entire document was set using an Apple Macintosh computer.

ISBN 0 9520246 1 6

British Library Cataloguing-in-Publication Data
A catalogue record for this book is available from the British Library.

After expenses have been met, any surplus arising from the sale (other than resale) of this book will be devoted to the Scottish Croquet Association.

Copies of this book may be purchased from

David Appleton, 4 Southwood Gardens, Newcastle upon Tyne, NE3 3BU, UK.

Preface

Some time ago David Appleton asked me to write a preface to a book he was producing. The profits (if any) were to go to the Scottish Croquet Association, and as its chairman I felt obliged to agree. My term of duty came to an end without any sign of the book and I breathed a sigh of relief, as one does when an opponent fails to hit in. My successor, who was in post for four years, also avoided the task. At last *The Lighter Side of Serious Croquet* is ready, but the current chairman is David himself, and he has pointed out that he can hardly write his own preface, so would I mind ... ? (I'll bet he edits it though!)

What can I say about the author/editor and his book? Although he plays serious croquet it is not always obvious that he plays croquet seriously. He does, however, take the enjoyment of the game seriously. Although, on a good day, he plays well, his main concern is that the experience should be pleasurable. Indeed he goes to great lengths to ensure this. A few years ago when he was going through one of those rough patches we all know about (he had reached the stage – or age – of *knowing* he was going to miss the next 3-yard roquet), he confided to me that he was consulting a hypnotherapist. This surprised me, until he explained that the therapy was not to help him hit the short roquets, but to help him get fun out of the game again. It worked. David now almost *prefers* missing roquets.

As the contents of this book show, David has other interests. For instance he does serious crosswords (but does he do them seriously?). Is it my imagination, or are his games on Sundays shorter than they are on Saturdays, so that he can fit in an attempt at Azed in the *Observer*? Not that he would try to solve it during play: he would never give such an impression of lack of interest in his opponent's game.

I knew David sang serious music (like Bach), but his attempt at writing it (page 29) is serious! Stick to composing crosswords, David.

David, a medical statistician, also plays at his work seriously. He has taken up my challenge to publish papers on croquet in both a medical journal and a statistical journal. He is half way there. ["May the best man win?" *The Statistician* 1995 volume 44 pp 529-538. You are right, Rod, I couldn't help editing even your preface.]

The Lighter Side of Serious Croquet is a pot-pourri of the sort of things (particularly Jack Shotton's fine cartoons) David finds amusing. I do too. But be warned: we are talking about the editor of the Scottish Croquet Association *Bulletin* whose caption to a picture of himself in national dress at the world championships was *The Kilt of the Personality.*

Rod Williams

Foreword

The decision to produce this book was made when Jack Shotton asked if I would like to look at some cartoons he had drawn. There were over a hundred and all well worth laughing at. Jack, Syd Jones and I used some of them in successive editions of our club magazine *Tyneside Croquet* between 1986 and 1989, and several have since appeared in the *Bulletin* of the Scottish Croquet Association and the CA's *Croquet Gazette* (sometimes known as *Croquet*). However, I always thought they deserved publication en masse, and I decided to mix them in with a medley of what I hope you will regard as other amusing croquet items, some of which I have borrowed from elsewhere, but most of which I have written myself. My aim was to emulate the much missed *Pick of Punch*.

It has taken a long time to finish *The Lighter Side*, and over the period of its production I have become indebted to many people who have helped. The contributors, of course: Jack Shotton; Bob Race for the crossword on page 11; Martin Kolbuszewski for his contributions to page 12 (as well as for having a name which in spite of all appearances is an anagram*); Rod Williams for his preface, for checking my answers to the refereeing quizzes, for two of the epitaphs on page 39, and not least for many great games as my partner for the SCA or as my opponent; Dorothy Rush for two of her many humorous articles (pages 16 and 34); Fred Mann for the poem on page 20; Gail Curry for her guide to artificial aids, first seen in her publication *Taking the Bisque*; the aforementioned Syd Jones for the puzzle on page 51; Denis Holland of NSW for the article on page 57; Mrs Stenhouse-Stewart of Maxwelton House who lent me the book described on page 80; and Robert Prichard, Andrew Gregory, Allan Ramsay and Malcolm O'Connell whose wit and humour I have reported in these pages. For anything which I have used without acknowledgement I apologise. (As far as I can ascertain the Tenniel drawings on pages 52 and 53 are not copyright.)

I had most help with the DIY articles, especially the technical drawings on pages 19, 41 and 63; Jack Shotton drew the originals, Nick and Joan Hoenich gave me access to ClarisDraw to computerise them, and Adrian Morley helped me realise the last of them in his workshop. John Matthews took the photographs on page 93.

I am also grateful to Chris Hudson for permission to use articles which appeared in the CA *Gazette* while he was editor. The editor of the SCA *Bulletin* was equally accommodating but, since that was me, gratitude is unnecessary. Finally, thanks to Rod (again) and Alex Murchie for their prof-leading skills. All those who have helped are entitled to the usual disclaimer: if there is anything herein which is wrong it is not their fault but mine alone.

* *of Uzbekistan silkworm*

Why choose the title I did? Well, I may not have played at the very top level, but I have played in the very best company. In the Home Internationals and other representative matches for Scotland, and in World and other Championships, I have played top players from Australia, England, France, Guernsey, Ireland, Japan, Jersey, New Zealand, South Africa, Switzerland, the United States and Wales. I can therefore legitimately claim to have played serious croquet, even though my desire to win in style has led to the accusation of not playing croquet seriously. Competition is all very well, but my real enjoyment comes from the occasions (in or out of matches) when the balls really obey me, and from interaction with other players. Many of the people I have met during my 11 seasons in the game are now good friends. If my biggest thrill was my first match in the Home Internationals when, in teeming Glasgow rain, I beat the English captain, close behind comes the very end of the 1994 season when on a lawn just vacated by players in a match between the Scottish and Irish Croquet Associations (so the hoops were ungenerous) I was pontificating to two of my team-mates about how one might set about a triple peel with only three balls. "Show us, then," they said – and I did!

I enjoy trying to persuade other people to play enterprising games, and that is why I have included some coaching articles in this book. They are designed for players of different standards, so most readers will find some too simple and some too advanced for their particular needs. In spite of the diagrams, only very experienced players will be able to follow the movement of the balls without a small lawn at their side. One of the first things I did when I took up croquet was to make a little green baize lawn on which I moved tiddleywinks the colour of croquet balls as I read Solomon and Cotter. Now I use magnetic boards in all my coaching courses, and would recommend all would-be serious players to buy themselves one.

Of course this book is not primarily for that sort of player: it is for those of any level of ambition and ability who play for fun. It is for all the people I have enjoyed playing, and all the ones I still look forward to meeting. I hope you enjoy it. If you don't then writing it has been even more self-indulgent than I thought!

David Appleton
Newcastle upon Tyne
January 1996

Contents

Items in italics are Jack Shotton's cartoons; there are more on pages 17, 23, 27, 38, 39, 57, 59, 60, 73, 86 & 87

Throughout this book the croquet balls are designated as follows:

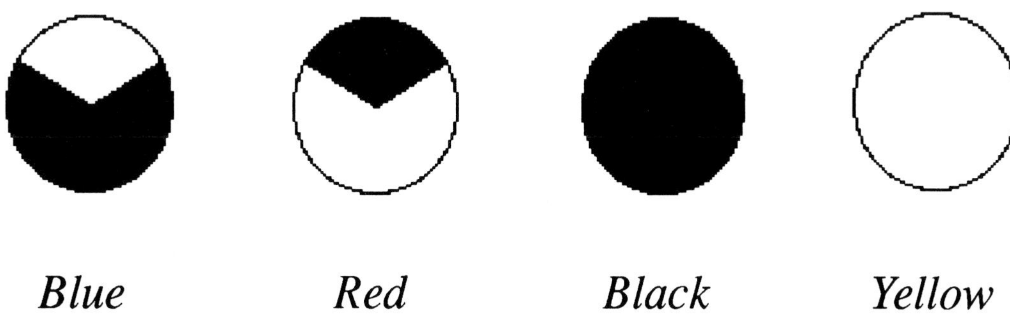

Duel in the sun

I don't know if I have ever told you about the time I saw Jeeves play croquet. No? Well, we were taking a moderately extended break from the rigours of Town life at Brinkley Court, Market Snodsbury, the rural establishment of my Aunt Dahlia and Uncle Tom, and it started, as so many things do, with a tiff between Madeline Bassett and her fiancé – my newt-fancying chum Gussie Fink-Nottle. The party of the first part had asserted to the party of the second part that the white butterflies in the rose garden were the tiny souls of poor dear dead little lambs, and having failed to elicit a sympathetic response, or indeed any response at all from the party of the second part, had retired to the terrace in what is, I believe, known as high dudgeon, though my Aunt Agatha would have been inclined to say that the gel was sulking.

Anyway, this rift in the lute, as I have heard Jeeves call such an estrangement, got to the ears of that blighter Roderick Spode, who marched up to Gussie and accused him of hurting Madeline's tender sensibilities. Gussie retorted that he thought he had shown commendable restraint in not telling Madeline she was a dreamy Gawd-help-us, and one thing leading to another in the way that it does, Spode ended up challenging old Gussie to a duel. Fortunately their rather heated exchanges had been conducted, at least on Spode's part, at some volume (Gussie having spent the latter part of the debate behind a solid mahogany door), and my Aunt Dahlia overheard and issued a nolle prosequi about the pistols-at-dawn stuff.

Madeline, however, was enchanted by the thought of a duel being fought over her, stamped her foot prettily and insisted on some sort of contest. Spode suggested croquet, of which he was, for some no doubt sadistic motive, inordinately fond. The game was in fact quite rife at Brinkley, and I had often heard Aunt Dahlia's penetrating contralto (which she had developed in her Quorn and Pytchley days) chide Uncle Tom for running hoops in the wrong direction. Indeed I had myself occasionally pottered about on the well manicured lawn (if a lawn may be so described), using the mallets and balls in Jeeves' words as occupation for an idle hour, but somehow the old grey matter could never quite get the hang of remembering in which order one was required to run the hoops.

Still, when Gussie, whose knowledge of croquet lagged substantially behind his knowledge of newts, stipulated that in a duel of this sort he should be allowed to choose a second, I immediately volunteered. Not only do we Woosters do our best to stand by our chums, I wanted to help the silly ass win and thereby enable him to hold his head high with the Bassett and at the same time pour oil on her ruffled feathers. For some reason she thinks I am batty about her, and if she should become short of a fiancé I could find myself perilously close to the long walk down the centre aisle at St Martin-in-the-Fields. What I didn't realise was that Gussie meant that we should play doubles. Spode was to partner my old adversary, the loony-doctor Sir Roderick Glossop, and in spite of our relative youth and the hand-eye co-ordination achieved by years of experience of pinching policemen's helmets on Boat Race night, the chances of us beating the two Roddies were about the same as Catsmeat Potter-Pirbright winning a bet against Oofy Prosser at the Drones. I felt that we were up against it, and did what I usually do in such circumstances. I sought out Jeeves, who was immersed in Spinoza.

"Jeeves," I said, "I feel we are up against it."

"Indeed, sir," replied that sage, raising an eyebrow perhaps a thirty-second of an inch at the urgency of my tone, and I hastened to lay the facts before him.

"Sir," he said, after giving the matter a moment's thought, "I judge that it would be more appropriate that a gentleman's personal gentleman should assist Mr Fink-Nottle, than that such a task should be carried out by a gentleman's personal gentleman's gentleman himself. Furthermore," he continued, "if the contest proves to be a consuming spectacle, it should be possible for you to slip away from the lawn and return Mr Travis's cow-creamer to its rightful display case."

I am sure I have enlightened you before about this dreadful artefact of Uncle Tom's. Jeeves calls it my albatross, but I can't for the life of me see why, because the bally thing is not only sadly lacking in charm, it is distinctly bovine in character. Be that as it may, it was agreed that Jeeves would espouse Gussie's cause, as the expression goes, and the following afternoon presented the unexpected sight of him (Jeeves that is, not Gussie) attired in white flannel trousers, flat-soled shoes and a panama hat, accompanying him (Gussie I mean) and bearing mallets onto the croquet lawn.

"Shall we play by Croquet Association rules, as for their Open Championships, gentlemen?" I heard Jeeves suggest quietly.

"Eh, what? Well, er, yes, naturally," blustered Spode.

"In that case, Sir Roderick, would you venture to forecast whether the reverse or obverse will be the uppermost face of this florin when it settles on the lawn subsequent to my projecting it in a vertical and trochilic fashion from my hand?"

When they had worked out that he meant to toss up, and they had settled a few more preliminaries, they were off.

A short croquet crossword by Dis

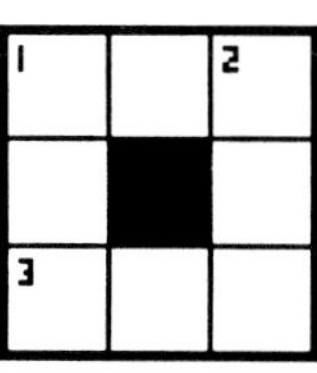

1 *ac.* Gentleman who, if he got a quad, would become someone to steer clear of.

3 *ac.* Help! What *do* you see in the reverse diagonal spread?

1 *dn.* Cheltenham maybe satisfies players' ambitions initially.

2 *dn.* I'm on the peg with blue; I'd be startled if the Scottish team took the lead.

Well, you know, it held my interest for a while, and we clapped politely when the odd hoop was made, but the sun was warm, and while no-one could blame the cold chicken consommé and suprème de fois gras au Champagne which Anatole had provided for lunch, I felt my concentration slipping and my eyelids gently closing. I suppose that if that young red-haired blister Bobbie Wickham hadn't fixed up my deck-chair to collapse, which it did after an hour or so of the Homeric struggle (if that's the chap I want), I would have followed the moves less closely. Once I had rearranged myself I could assess the progress made by the players by means of some jolly little clips on the hoops which show how far each ball has got. Dashed clever idea to use them like that: Bingo Little and I used to attach them to our ties to remind ourselves which balls we were playing.

Anyway, I could tell that all was not well. Jeeves had yet to make a hoop, and Gussie had only made 5, while Spode and Sir Roderick had 7 apiece. Jeeves seemed to be on the lawn quite a lot, but going in all directions except towards his hoop, then the others would have a biff, then Gussie would try to make the hoop with his little yellow clip on it, usually managing to progress about half way through. It would be nice to think that Gussie's strength was as the strength of ten because his heart was pure, as I have heard Jeeves put it, but his strength seemed equal only to hitting the ball about two inches less than was necessary. The only hope was that luck would favour Gussie's side, and there did seem to be a glimmer of that, because after Spode was three times in five minutes prevented from hitting Sir Roderick's ball by the intervention of a nearby hoop he so lost his temper as to throw his mallet into the hedge.

When battle had been joined for getting on for two hours, and the sun seemed to be standing still in the midst of heaven and hasting not to go down, just as it did upon Gibeon in the day when the Lord delivered up the Amorites before the children of Israel, they brought out tea. Anatole had provided Gussie with special French mustard for his sandwiches, but he still looked as if life was a journey we all have to gang, and care is the burden we carry alang (as some poet, possibly the poet Burns, observes). Jeeves, however, came as near as he ever does to seeming to enjoy himself, though where the pleasure came from I couldn't guess. Sir Roderick had now run all the twelve hoops required of him, Spode had just been successful with his tenth, and although in some fashion Gussie had contrived to achieve 9, Jeeves had yet to open his account. I sympathised with his misfortune, but forbore to tell the chap that he should have let the young master play after all. We Woosters can refrain from twisting the k in the w when we have to. Indeed I slipped off in the general hoohah of the tea things being removed and the match restarting, to replace the bally cow-creamer, and so it was that I missed the sensational development.

Instead of starting again with about a 30-yard shot, Jeeves had calmly picked up his ball, placed it a yard from Spode's and played from there. Spode had of course attempted to intervene, but Jeeves had merely replied "Law 36(a)(2), sir," presented him with a little book of rules and continued. I think Gussie must have exaggerated about what then transpired, for if he is to be believed Jeeves proceeded to make all of his hoops while contriving to knock Gussie's through the three that remained for it. Certainly it is true that when I returned sans cow-creamer Sir Roderick's visage had taken on the hue of his blue ball (with a sort of purplish tinge) and Spode's was blacker than his black one. Jeeves was in the process of guiding his ball through the red-topped hoop, which my memory correctly identified as the last one required, and he then encouraged his and Gussie's balls onto the peg in the middle of the lawn.

"Plus four, I believe, gentlemen," he murmured. "Thank you for an entertaining game. Well played, Mr Fink-Nottle, sir."

I didn't manage to talk to Jeeves privately until I was putting on the old soup and fish. It turns out that before his present holiday entertainment of shrimping at Bognor he used to go to Budleigh Salterton and play croquet.

"I usually manage to visit Cheltenham whenever your travels take you to Gloucestershire, Mr Wooster, and the exigencies of attending to you allow. There is a particular person with whom I play there. One could not, I am afraid, sir, call him a gentleman, but we have had some interesting encounters."

"And what was all that at the end, Jeeves?"

"It is called a triple peel, sir; I once saw Mr Solomon defeat Mr Cotter with a similar manoeuvre at Budleigh."

"Well Jeeves," I said, "it sounds more like a term from campo... campa..."

"Campanology, sir?"

"Precisely so, Jeeves. I never did get the hang of croquet terminology. Aunt Dahlia is more likely to bellow 'yoicks' than anything else when she runs a hoop."

Just then the dinner gong rang and I trickled downstairs; cucumber sandwiches are all very well, but Anatole was giving us croquettes de veau cordon bleu avec piments rouges et jaunes, and a rather drinkable Pinot Noir.

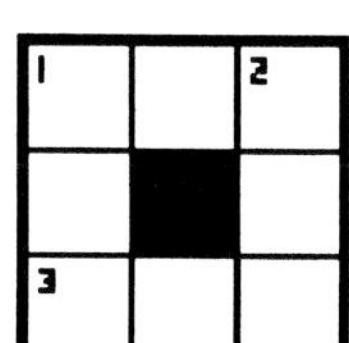

A short croquet crossword by Dis

1 *ac.* This is a feature of most Easter tournaments – and late autumn ones.

3 *ac.* A good stroke? Or a duff?

1 *dn.* After time Prince takes lead in Opens with high-risk manoeuvre.

2 *dn.* It's a breeze! But it it would be risky if Henry went round with yellow.

Great moments in history

If we're going to play this game, you're going to have to!

Would you mind not inventing fire with my mallets.

I said "build me a wooden horse then fetch me my mallet".

Should we report this to the NASA or the CA?

Coaching tips #1
How to crosswire your opponent

When the occasion arises (usually in a handicap game, but occasionally when playing to advanced rules), it is very satisfying to crosswire your opponent at hoop 1 and lay up with a rush from corner III, as in Fig 1. It is rather less satisfying to get such a leave wrong, either by failing to place the balls properly for the crosswire or, even more embarassing, to leave no ball open and allow your opponent a lift to your balls in baulk. So let us see how you can increase your chances of doing it properly.

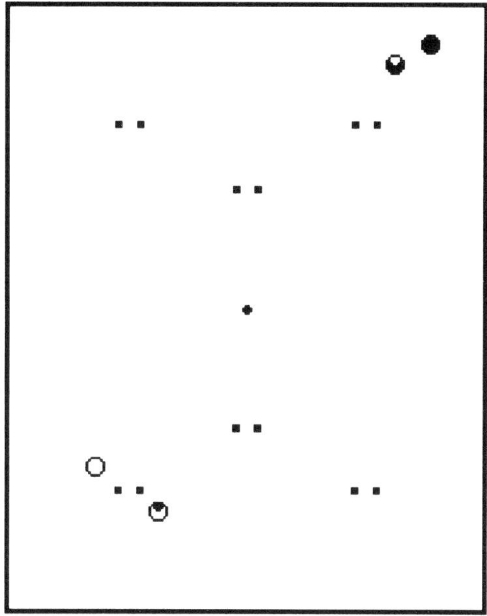

Fig 1

I am going to assume that you are in control at penultimate with your partner ball as pivot and a good pioneer at rover. If you haven't managed to gain that amount of control during your break, then forget about the crosswire: you're only likely to mess it up. Do something boring, but realistic, like putting a ball at each of the first two hoops and laying up in corner IV.

Let's suppose you are playing with blue, making penultimate off red, yellow is at rover, and black (still for hoop 1) is a pivot 4 or 5 yards south-west of the peg (see Fig 2). Run your hoop trying to give yourself a rush to about point ① from where you can croquet red to ③ with a little drive or stop-shot which leaves blue at ②.

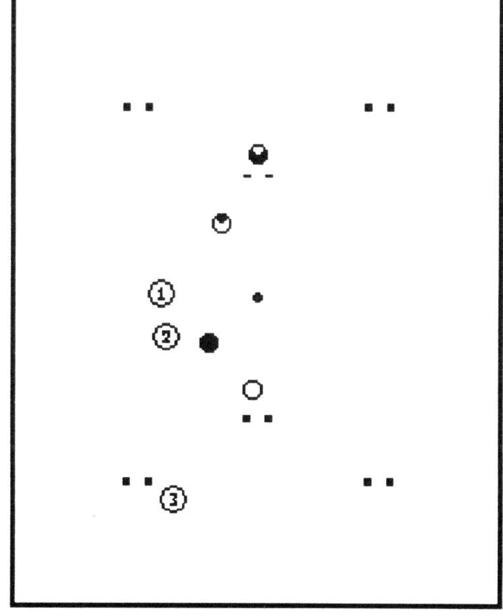

Fig 2

Now rush black a little to the east so that you can croquet it to point ④ going to yellow (Fig 3), making the hoop so that you can rush the pilot to ⑤ (Fig 4); this is a position from which you can place the yellow accurately to ⑥, as nearly wired from red as you can, and still get blue into a position beside red from

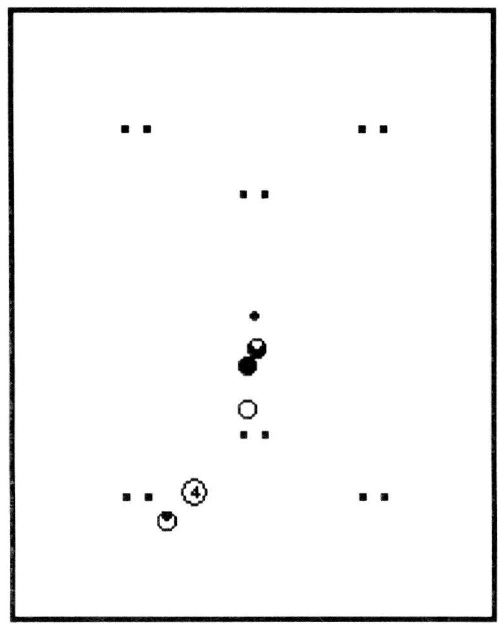

Fig 3

which you can gently roquet it straight to retain the wired position if you have achieved it, or to either side to complete the wiring if you need to (Fig 5). You don't want to have to play much of a split shot when you position the yellow, but at the same time you don't want the hoop or the other two balls to be in the way.

How far from the hoop should the balls be? I suggest between 2 and 3 feet is about right. The closer you can put the yellow the greater your margin of error for the red; but of course if you leave it short of the hoop you are in trouble! Don't be tempted to try to rush the yellow into position and then come back to sort out the red; a croquet shot is much more secure and gives you more flexibility. And do remember that just because the red can't roquet yellow it doesn't mean that yellow can't hit red. Check the required

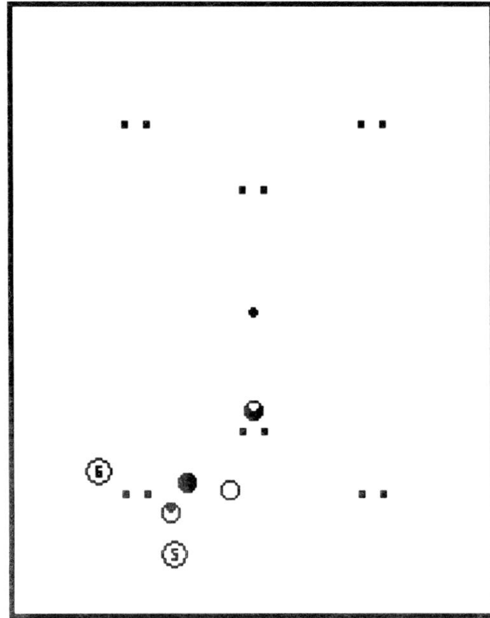

Fig 4

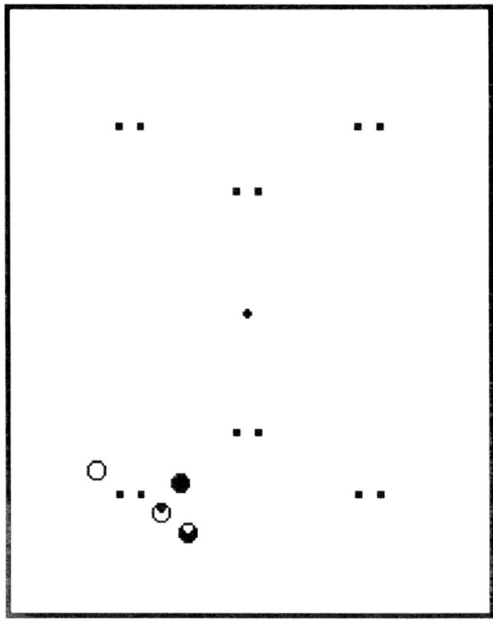

Fig 5

position for the red carefully from both sides of the hoop.

There are still some dangers, so don't relax completely just because the balls are crosswired. You have yet to play a little take-off from the red, just nudging it along the wiring line, to get a rush on black to near corner III. The position of the partner ball is really quite crucial: it must be far enough from the red so that there is no chance of a hampered stroke, yet it must be near enough that the rush is still possible even if some final positioning of the red precludes the desired take-off. And then there is the final moment in corner III. The reason we have crosswired the balls north-west to south-east of hoop 1 is to make it possible for each of them to see either the black or the blue, but preferably not both, and certainly not a double target. It is probably slightly easier to arrange the crosswire south-west to north-east, but then it is more difficult to avoid wiring the farther ball completely or leaving a hampered backswing for the nearer one. You want to make sure that the long shot is easily picked up if it is missed, and that you have enough room to stop it to hoop 2 and still rush the blue into pivot position. At the same time you want a rush out of the corner if the shot is refused. On anything but a very fast court the rush to hoop 2 is probably safer than trying to aim for corner I. See Fig 1 again, but note that because the hoops and balls on the diagram are not to scale it is impossible to tell when balls at a distance are wired; only practising on the lawn will show you exactly where you want to leave the balls.

And practise precision: choose the blade of grass the ball should rest on.

Just one more thing: you obviously don't have much margin for error if you crosswire west to east, and it is tempting to veer towards the north-south direction. Don't let your opponent run his hoop with one of his balls, though. I can assure you from sad experience that the spectators will laugh!

I said at the beginning that this tactic could sometimes be employed in an advanced game. Have you thought of an appropriate occasion? One such is this. You were going round with your second (black) ball, having done one peel of your triple, when you were hampered after 1-back (annoying, but the hoops were very tight). Your opponent did rather better, but ended up on B-baulk after missing a hampered shot at blue after 4-back. He had left yellow by rover, having bounced it off the wire in attempting a peel after 3-back, and your black was his pioneer for penultimate. Now you have a choice of lifting black and taking it to the peg — not too difficult as the ball at rover is a reasonable pioneer for 2-back — or playing with blue. This is a case when you should use the forward ball: take it to the peg, arrange the crosswire as above (except that the black and red start in transposed positions), and finish when your opponent misses or refuses the long shot. Taking the backward ball to the peg concedes a lift, and trying to avoid it by finishing with a double peel is rather too optimistic even by my standards.

International section.

English: a crosswire at rover.

French: un télégramme faché au vagabond.

Technical terms

I said to rush it to four-back!

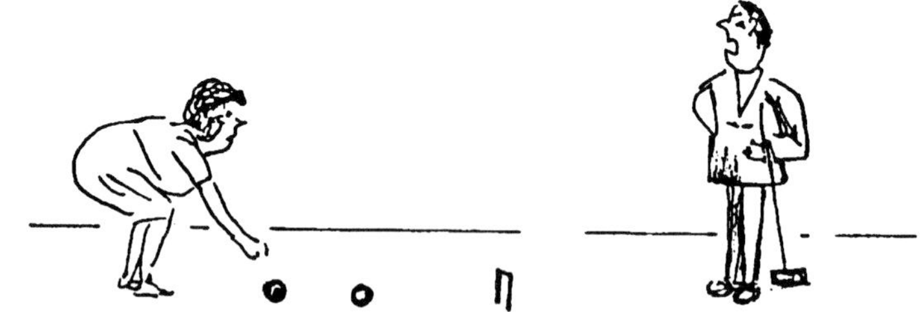

No, woman! I said you had a gift there.

No, Mabel. I said "you're wired".

A croquet crossword

by
Bob Race

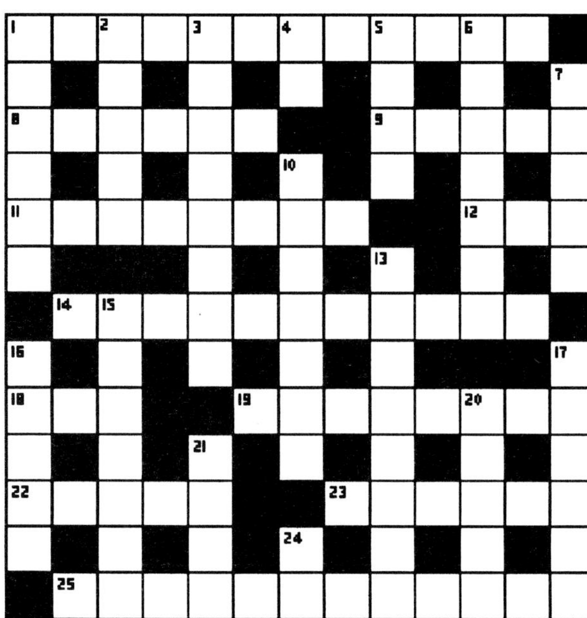

Across

1. It's his protection, when it comes to the test, from crazy mob at corners. (12)
8. If poor they may give away the innings, a hazard late in the season. (6)
9. Cold briefly, then warm — not in a Croquet Club I trust! (5)
11. Say I feel poorly, but not to the Tournament Manager. (4,4)
12,14, Entirely circular fractures are much to be desired. (3,5,6)
14. See 12.
18. Give yourself one on the back if you never double this back. (3)
19. Little Bella's Miss Wodehouse unwilling to attempt a break. (4,4)
22. Get a grip, 18! (5)
23. Twisting twisted necklace earns a croquet shot. (6)
25. The ultimate achievement for the remains of half a dozen oranges? (8,4)

Down

1. Croquet Club? (6)
2. Tuition group for girl with 16 bisques? (5)
3. Or not yet finished? 19's games tend to be. (8)
4. The end of Croquet for alien visitor. (1,1)
5. A temptation in frost, ice or snow. (4)
6. The first in a 25 — that's half enough. (7)
7. Approach your ball from behind, it bears fruit. (5)
10. One way to make 6 if you are black, red or yellow. (3,4)
13. Chances against a 25 just before lunch? (3,2,3)
15. Open University's diet upset the partners not in play. (3,4)
16,21. Shares out ill-gotten fisherman's weights. (5,4)
17. Thrash learner (pale coloured). (6)
20. Timid creature initially makes our usual score easily. (5)
21. See 16.
24. Raised President's Cup: CID's present for removal. (2)

(Solution on page 89.)

A place by any other name

Whenever I set out from Newcastle to play croquet in Glasgow or Southport I pass a signpost to Peelwell. Maybe this is why I feel that placenames should mean something. More likely I am influenced by Douglas Adams and John Lloyd's book *The Meaning of Liff* in which they attach definitions of common objects and activities to place names. For example, "a piece of wood used to stir paint and thereafter stored uselessly in a shed in perpetuity" is a **Cotterstock** (Northants), while **Fulking** (Sussex) is "pretending not to be in when the carol-singers come round".

At any rate, on one occasion I felt moved to write to *Croquet* with a selection which included the following:

Acaster Malbis (interj, Yorkshire): expression indicative of the unavailing use of a bisque;
Bentpath (interj, Dumfriesshire): the ball has just deviated from the trajectory on which I unerringly sent it and has failed to achieve a simple 30-yard roquet;
Broad Laying (n, Hampshire): a double target;
Clubworthy (adj, Cornwall): 1) having a handicap of 18 or less;
2) (of hoop position) about 4 yards away at an angle;
East Blatchington (n, Sussex): inability to hit the short lift shot;
West Wittering (n, Sussex): inability to hit the tice.

I also pointed out the inadvisability of using the third of these in the USA.

I was delighted when Martin Kolbuszewski replied in kind. In line with our increasing links with Europe, his offering included the following places in France:

Ardennes (vb, North East): what the ground does in dry weather;
Biscarosse (adj, Gascony): disappointed after taking a bisque only to miss a 2-foot roquet;
Carcassone (adj, Roussillon): very accurate (lit. dead on);
Homps (n pl, Roussillon): hills with hoops on;
Toulon (adj, Provence): of a take-off which goes off the lawn;
Toulouse (vb, Languedoc): to see your opponent pegging out.

Martin also added for good measure **Toulouse-Lautrec** (vb): to forget which hoop you are on. But perhaps that is enough, because he also included:
Prat (n, Roussillon): compiler of glossaries of croquet jargon.

How good a referee are you?

(answers on page 86)

1. Dan has a lift. He places his ball in corner 2 and makes a roquet on his partner ball about 4 yards away. His opponent points out that he has not played from baulk, and you are called on to determine how play should continue. What is your decision?

2. You have been called on to attend the peg as Steve attempts to peg out his opponent from some distance. The opponent's ball misses the peg and goes off the lawn; the striker's ball hits the peg, but you are not sure whether this occurred before or after the other ball left the lawn. Should the striker's ball be removed from the lawn?

3. Ray roquets black with red and takes croquet from it, sending black off the lawn. Red ends up within the yard line area with a rush on blue. After replacing black on the yardline Ray indicates that he will take a bisque. May he play red from where it lies?

4. Willie and Frank both play off 8. They are drawn to play each other in both the handicap and the class event, and during the game they discover that Willie has been told by the manager that they were playing in the handicap, whereas Frank had read on the list of matches that it was the class event. The manager calls on you to adjudicate. Frank is on 2 and penult, but Willie is only on 3 and 4. What do you decide?

5. In an advanced doubles game Bill and Ben, playing blue and black respectively, are entitled to a lift under law 36(a). After much discussion with his partner, Bill picks up black and plays it from the end of A baulk. He misses, and replaces the ball on the yardline beside red. His opponents then realise that Ben should have been playing black. Do the balls stay as they lie? Should Ben play the lift shot? Should Bill take the lift with the blue? Or what?

6. Red roquets black. In walking to collect red, the striker accidentally kicks black. What provision is made for this in the laws?

7. Syd misses a roquet in a corner. He takes a bisque and plays with the ball which was already in the corner. He makes two hoops with it, using two more bisques, before the error is discovered. What happens?

8. Charlie clangs a hoop and takes a bisque. He effects a roquet, gets poor position with the croquet stroke and gives the situation earnest thought. At long last he attempts the hoop and fails again. He looks at the balls from all angles and eventually hits his ball into a corner. His opponent says "you have taken a bisque, you know". Is this correct? If you have been observing the vignette can you do anything?

9. At the end of a turn which began when he took a half bisque, Vic ends up in the jaws of his hoop, having trickled there in taking position. Can he take a bisque and complete the running of the hoop? Can he run the hoop in a subsequent turn if he finds it still there?

10. A referee is called to a distant court by Chris, who complains that Alex has committed a fault (a double tap) approaching a hoop. Alex disagrees. What are the powers of the referee?

The Marathon

for those long drawn out matches.

The Kater

for use if weather conditions change from mild to bitter during a turn.

Jack's

The Offset

will go where no other mallet head will go. Ideal for close hoop work.

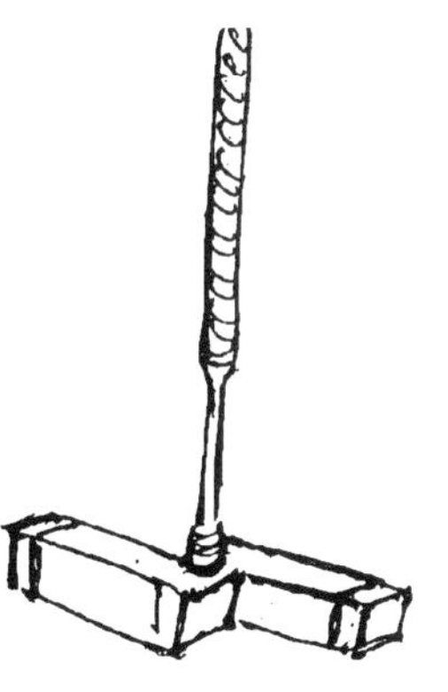

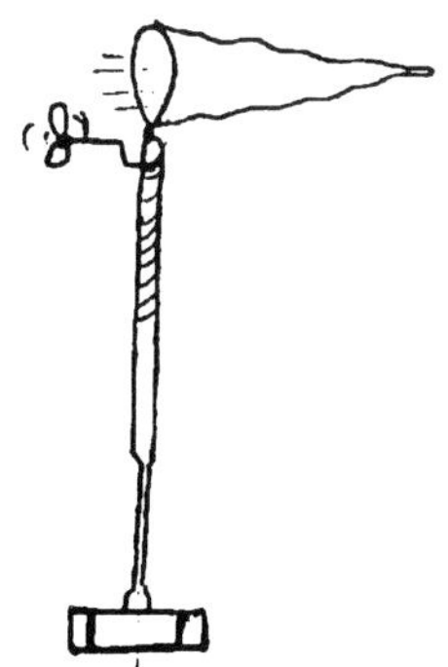

The Socker

for the player who has everything. Gives wind speed and direction before attempting that long shot.

Mallets

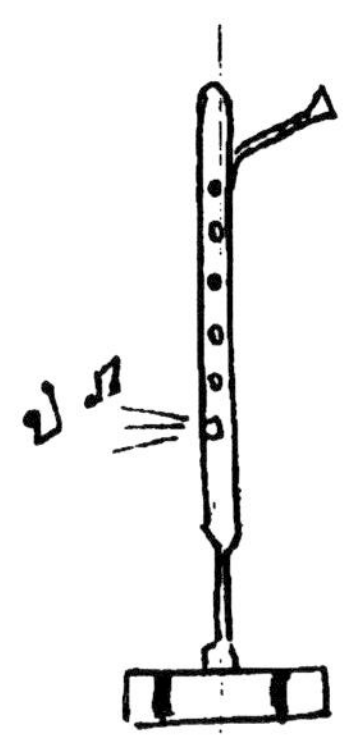

The Entertainer

Keep the spectators amused
while you wait your turn.

The Replay

Snap your opponent in the act.
Did the ball move?
Was it a crush shot?
Snap it and see.

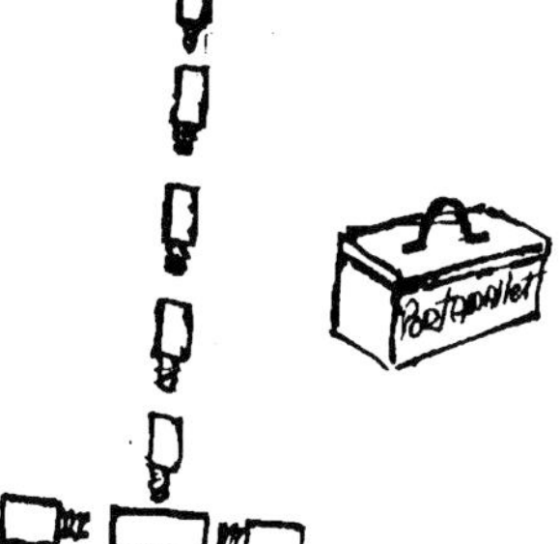

The Portamallet

in 8 parts, complete with case

The Emily Pankhurst

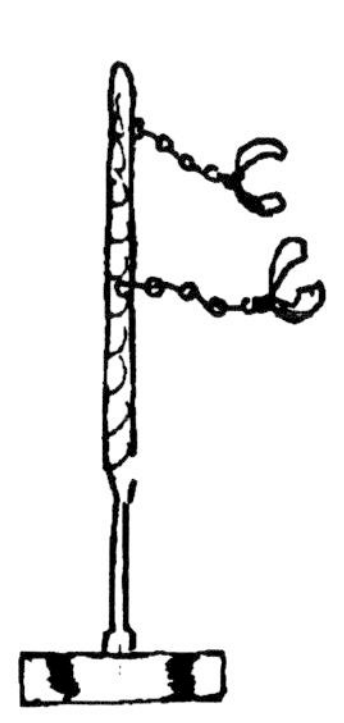

for the croquet widow.
Keep him at home with this unique attachment by
chaining yourself to his favourite mallet.

Winning with Rush

by Dorothy Rush

Part 12 : Tactics

Your opponent is for peg and peg. He has put you in first and third corners and has laid up in the fourth corner with a rush to the middle of the lawn. You are for 1 and 3. What do you do?

In these circumstances the beginner or middle-bisquer is often at a loss, whereas the A-class player will step confidently onto the lawn and do just the right thing. (Remember: many a game has been won ...) The A-class player can do this because he is more experienced than the B or C-class player. And what, you may well ask, would he do in the circumstances described above? What, in fact, should you, the middle-bisquer do? The answer has the simplicity of true brilliance: you must hit in.

Take another, very different situation: your opponent has seized the innings and gone to 4-back. His leave is a text-book NSL and you know he has triples for breakfast every morning. What now? Again the A-class player knows immediately what the answer is: hit the lift.

Now this is all very well, and my readers will be wondering if I have reduced the intricacies of croquet to an all-too-basic brutality. Is there nothing else to joining the A class? Lord, yes! The subtleties of this croquet of ours lies somewhere between chess and snooker, or so we are told. It's not just banging balls around. So ... what to do when you have the innings and a break is unfolding before you. Again the A-class player has it over the lesser mortal. His tactic is again devastatingly simple: don't break down.

"Och aye, easy peasy," I hear you cry — assuming a Scots accent for some unfathomable reason — "so how dae I dae tha'?" Again the answer is — to the A-class player — child's play. (Remember: to minus players croquet is a very easy game. I sometimes wonder why they bother with such a boringly simple activity. Could it be they are after those nice little trips abroad?) Yes ... well ... how not to break down was the subject under discussion. Here the essential tactic is: get on the correct side of the hoop.

"Hang on," you say; you having read Solomon and been on a weekend course. "You mean in front of and six inches away. Isn't that what sets the minus player apart from the rest of us?" No, dear, it's not: I said 'on the correct side' and that's what I meant. Once there, bang the ball through. It will end up in prime position for the forward rush you require (unless, perchance, you need a rush to the side, in which case it will oblige accordingly) — or it will if your handicap is low enough.

"I see," you whisper in awe. "And what sort of shot do I play; a firm stroke or a gentle tap?" You haven't been paying attention, have you? I said 'bang it through'. Just bang it through. Now I hope you have got all that, because I'm now moving on to the deeper intricacies of croquet tactics.

These are mostly verbal, and their value lies in their being available for use at all times, even when your opponent is in play or has just seized the innings. There is not space here to elaborate fully on their use, but one example should suffice. You have laid a complicated trap for your opponent; if she makes the text-book response you are in with a fair chance of getting a break. She, rash woman, does entirely the wrong thing, puts your plan in jeopardy and threatens to regain the innings if you foul up your next manoeuvre. How do you regain the upper hand here?

Skill is not enough. Leave your mallet where it is; climb slowly out of your chair, shaking your head gently, sadly even, and approach your opponent as she leaves the lawn. If necessary detain her with a friendly hand: "I can't agree with your tactics there, Mary/Jane/Deborah. Not with the lift pending. I really don't think you should have done that."

Pick up your mallet and resume your innings with confidence. You have done enough to ensure victory. After the game you may enlarge upon the theme of your opponent's tactics, thus ensuring that, when next you meet, you have the upper hand.

You are now ready to join the A class.

Some people will stoop to anything to intimidate their opponents.

Gadgetry for beginners

How to make a CATAPULT

Many croquet players, during the winter months, turn into handymen. But instead of making up for the neglect they have lavished on their houses throughout summer weekends, they make croquet equipment. Some go as far as making mallets or balls; others invent new kinds of carrots to make hoops stay firmer in sandy soil. Most of us, however, have more modest aims and less advanced workshops, though such deficiencies give scope for much misguided ingenuity. Here I shall show how you can make a device for testing whether or not a ball near the boundary is in fact on or off the lawn. You will need only a saw, a drill and a screwdriver, though it is true that it would be useful if the saw was an electric one with which you could cut an arc of a circle. (If you are like me, you will also need a supply of plastic wood and elastoplast, so don't think you need to be an expert).

I hear some muted muttering among you enquiring why you can't just look at the ball and decide with the naked eye, and I reply that that is all very well – though parallax can be deceptive – but it doesn't answer the real question, which is: what are you going to do with the long winter evenings after you have studied Wylie and practised your swing in front of the wardrobe mirror?

First you need to ferret around in your garage for some chipboard, preferably white. You need one piece approximately 17" by 7½" and two pieces each 6" by 7½" though the dimensions are not crucial. You also need about 10" of piano hinge (which the old upright in the lounge will probably never miss), a few screws, and a couple of magnetic catches which can be obtained from the local DIY store of your choice.

The drawing on the opposite page will guide you, and there is a photograph of the finished article in use on page 93. It is important that the wood is accurately rectangular, at least at what is going to be the bottom, so if possible use the original edges there. When you have assembled your CATAPULT (Contraption Able To Alleviate Problems Under Law Ten) closing it should leave the bottom edges exactly level. Nothing else is critical, except that there should be plenty of room for the arch to pass over a ball. To achieve true elegance you should cover any bare edges of your chipboard with matching adhesive strips, and for a really professional touch, to allow equal ease of testing of light and dark coloured balls, the two sides of the inside of the arch should be in contrasting dark and light colours.

All that remains is to learn to use your CATAPULT. There are two methods, depending on whether the boundary is of string or whitewash. If the former, use your CATAPULT *vertically*. Gently slide the middle section towards the boundary from *inside* the court, taking care to move neither the string nor the ball, keeping the ball under the arch. When the device and the string are in contact along the length of the middle section lie on the ground (don't move the string!) and see whether the ball protrudes through the arch.

If the boundary lines are whitewashed it is better to use this versatile device *horizontally*. Unfold it completely and, from the *outside* of the court, push it towards the ball until its whole length touches the inside of the line. The arch should be on the side farthest from the ball and the middle of one of the flaps should be level with the ball. Close that flap; if it touches the ball then the ball was off the lawn. If you can't move the flap turn the CATAPULT over and try again.

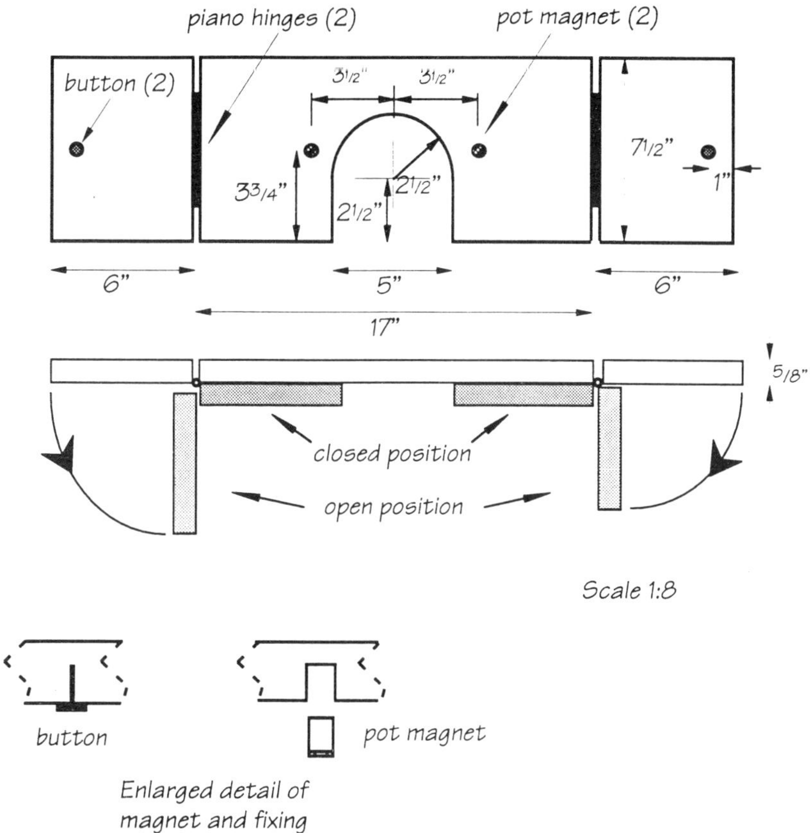

Should you make a really good job of your CATAPULT you might like to refine it. For instance you can increase its adaptability by painting religious pictures on it and using it as a triptych.

Where is this?

If you want to play croquet that's chaoghaire in a club where the crack's never draoghaire, you'll find life proceeds geilidh – a continual ceilidh – just a mile or two west of Dun Laoghaire.

Carrickmines

Fred's page

This page is dedicated to Fred Mann, secretary of the Scottish Croquet Association. The poem is by him, and the crosswords are for him. They may not be as hard as the *Listener* crosswords which he does by the side of the lawn while his opponent is playing a break, but perhaps they will pass those awkward moments when he is waiting for a referee to arrive from a distant lawn to watch him play a hampered stroke.

The six-foot roquet

When I was a 4
I was nerveless and sure.

At $4^1/_2$
I could miss and still laugh.

When I was 5
Doubts would arrive.

When I was 6
I developed tics.

When I was 7
To hit one was heaven.

And now I am 8
And resigned to my fate.

A short croquet crossword by Dis

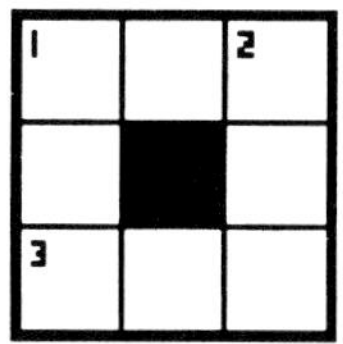

1 *ac.* Old leave. In baulk?
3 *ac.* Peg out; it may be impressive.
1 *dn.* I judge, slightly strangely, the indoor game loses nothing.
2 *dn.* Duffer, perhaps, losing head in crucial match.

(Solutions to all the short croquet crosswords are on page 90.)

A short croquet crossword by Dis

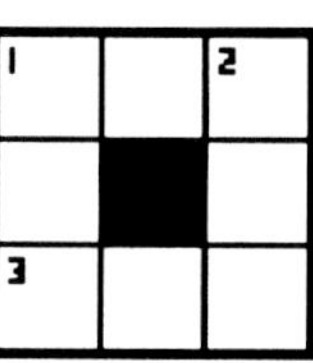

1 *ac.* There's trouble as Ms Curry loses touch of genius.
3 *ac.* Triple ends in rover peel failure leaving a heap of rubbish.
1 *dn.* Take contact, but lift head and lose on time; it's part of the drama.
2 *dn.* Once round, partner goes round.

Triumph

Looks like Phillpot has won again.

You're next on lawn 3 against Jones. You can't mistake him: he's oozing with confidence.

He keeps having these crazy spells when he wants to give up croquet.

Another whitewash. How come, if all the world's a stage, all the clowns play for our team?

and disaster

Coaching tips #2

You in your small corner, and I in mine

In *Ellicott and the Triple Peel* DK Holland mentions the leave where all of the balls are in different corners (see page 58). This is not just a pretty conceit; it is a very effective leave when you are giving bisques and you feel that your opponent is being rather generously treated. I suffered it once (at the hands of Keith Aiton) when I was 4-handicap and he was -2. On winning the toss I had chosen the balls, and with a briefly raised eyebrow my opponent put me in, hit on the fourth turn, and went round. I tried to shoot down the west boundary, but went off about 10 yards from my partner ball in corner I. Completely put out I refused to take a bisque. Keith missed the 26-yard shot out of corner IV by a whisker; there is very little doubt that if he had hit I would have lost with all my 6 bisques standing. As it was I got the corner cannon, went round using only one bisque and left him cross-wired at hoop one and laid up near second corner, having failed to get a good rush to corner III. I was later chastised (quite rightly) for not taking a bisque to lengthen the shot from about 27 yards to 33 yards. I was lucky, because again the shot was narrowly missed, and I won without using any of my remaining bisques. However, I learned one lesson more clearly from that game than from many I had lost: if your opponent is likely to win in two turns don't give him chances when your bisques allow you not to.

I am not going to tell you what I should have done after my opponent's leave, partly because I am still not sure, and partly because I have to be able to confuse my opponents occasionally. I have no intention of giving *all* my secrets away. Instead I shall give a brief

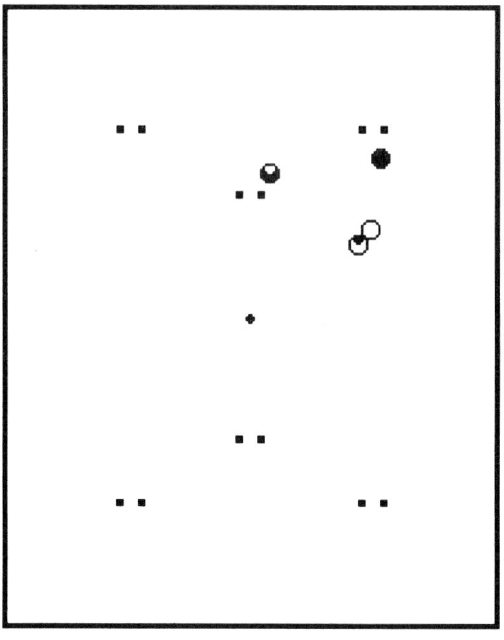

description of one way of arranging this attractive leave. I shall suppose you are playing with red, and have reached the position shown in the figure, that is: you have just run 3-back, have sent blue to penult as a pioneer, and are about to take croquet from yellow before making 4-back off black.

Croquet yellow to a position about a couple of yards south-west of corner III, and run 4-back with a rush into the corner. (You will find attempting this leave good practice for getting rushes out of hoops.) If you manage to rush into the corner – and we are talking about an 8-yard rush with a margin of error of about 2 feet on either side, so there is a very good chance– take off gently from black to get a rush on yellow to north-east of penult, from where you put it to rover as a pioneer. Err, if anything, on being long and to the east. If you failed to rush black into corner III you will have to improvise a bit; I shall tell you what to do when we reach the next corner, where it is even more likely you will have to.

Make penult with a rush to the south boundary near, but not in or *too* near, corner IV; about two yards away is best, but other positions close by are not impossible (yet!). Take off to your pioneer at rover, leaving blue on the south yard-line. Make rover with a rush to corner IV.

Now, this rush is a bit longer and you might not get yellow right in the corner. If you do, take off to get a rush on blue to corner I; if you don't, then play a croquet stroke to put yellow into the corner and get your rush on blue. Remember that yellow is put on the corner spot before you can take your rush on blue, and it mustn't get in the road; that's why blue shouldn't be left too near the corner. Rush the blue as near corner I as you can get it, croquet it into the corner, and all you have to do is hit the red straight enough to get it the 33 yards into corner II. All the balls will be sitting beside their matching corner flags.

Remember that if you don't get it quite right, and miss one of the corners by a foot, you give your opponent the opportunity of shooting at that ball, and getting a very easy rush out if he misses and takes a bisque. And, of course, rolling one of the balls off the lawn with another close by isn't such brilliant defence either. Just don't blame me if you mess it up and lose, but it's splendidly satisfying to get it right, even if it's your last contribution to the game.

If I ever get out of this mess, they can keep my coaching badge.

Despising wind and rain and fire

Weather conditions loom large with croquet players. The game loses much of its appeal in rain, when you can't even sit down while your opponent plays, or high winds, when your cucumber sandwiches blow away. The gentleman on the weather vane can be encountered at Budleigh Salterton, and the lady is at the Kelburn Croquet Club in Wellington, New Zealand — a beautifully flat part of what must be the hilliest city in the croquet-playing world.

The flooded lawns are not typical of Scottish HQ at Bush, just south of Edinburgh, but they did the author a good turn, because he won his first open tournament when play was abandoned with them in this condition!

But for real problems, have a look at Rotorua Croquet Club; the sulphurous fumes don't actually come up through the hoop holes, but it's close. One might certainly imagine "the deil had business on his hand."

Domestic bliss

I'll give you just another minute to decide who's going to take the shot before I contact the marriage guidance council.

I still think the blue ball looks better over there.

And I say it's my ball.

Betty, are you sure you haven't seen my mallet anywhere?

Gail's guide to artificial aids

The most comprehensive consumer guide ever printed

Some players try to get through a weekend tournament using only their skill with a mallet, but it pays to be adept with other equipment too. Here Gail Curry, winner of the Barlow Bowl in 1991, 92 & 93, and of the Women's Championship in 1992 & 93 (and maybe some other years – she doesn't always remember to tell me) explains the advantages of some other items.

Spectacles. These have always been the most popular aid for the older player, and it used to be felt that they were beyond reproach and simply allowed the visually impaired to participate in croquet along with their more able-bodied colleagues. They were regarded with no more disapprobation than bisques. However, in recent times, due to great improvements in spy merchandise, spectacles may not be as innocent as they seem. Some of the most sophisticated pairs are believed to use microdot technology to allow the player to read the CA coaching manual. A petition was recently sent to the World Croquet Federation demanding the testing of all spectacles prior to competitive games. Unfortunately, most of the council members wore spectacles and the petition was ignored. The only really safe way of checking your opponent's glasses is to try them for yourself; if they refuse you know they have something to hide.

Price: from about £25; look out for exciting 2-for-1 deals, and special offers of 1-hour assembly.
Value for money: ☆☆☆☆ when dry, ☆ when raining.

Gail Curry *the* outplayer

Contact lenses. A fairly new invention, these are beginning to replace some of the more cumbersome spectacles. The real advantages of this product are that they are not affected by the British weather, and they are difficult to spot whilst in use. Their only drawback seems to be that if you drop them they are difficult to find and you have to grovel round on your hands and knees. This, of course, does offer opportunities to move critically positioned balls.
Price: from £35; value for money ☆☆☆.

Sunglasses. One of the commonest aids used. The recommended best buy is the aviator mirrored-lens type, as not only will they keep the sun out of your eyes, but you can use them to dazzle your opponents when they are in play. There are two drawbacks: they either end up lost or broken, and you usually play with a wrong ball – frequently belonging to one of the double-bankers – as they filter out not only sunlight but colour.
Price: £4.99; value ☆☆.

The Sweeper

For removing worm casts and cigarette ends during a break

Waterproof clothing. Although this is used predominantly to keep the wearer dry in wet conditions, it offers two further advantages. The nylon variety is particularly effective in acutely annoying some players by means of a grating rasping noise reminiscent of a six-foot tall cicada. But the real gain for unscrupulous players is that it is often possible to have a better player play instead of you, because most waterproofs have a substantial element of camouflage.
Price: from £12; value for money ☆☆☆.

Sunday papers. These present many opportunities to the inventive user. Even the tabloid variety can be used to conceal a copy of Wylie's *Expert Croquet Tactics*, while the 'quality' papers can even take a large magnetic board for helping with tactical decisions. In addition these contain crosswords, which can either be used as a time-wasting aid by pretending that you were not aware that your opponent's turn had ended, or – better still – as a way of breaking your opponent's concentration. You merely tell him you are having problems with a clue (preferably one for which you have entered some incorrect letters in the diagram), and he will a) not watch you carefully while you are playing, and b) possibly even forget he is playing you.
Price: about £1; value ☆☆☆☆.

Personal stereo players. Perhaps the most controversial aid of recent times. Due to the appliance of science there are now radios, cassette players and compact disc players available either to act as calming influences, play coaching material, or block out distracting noises – such as your opponent trying to forestall play, or a double banker trying to get you to move out of his way.
Price: from £10; value ☆☆☆☆☆.

Cigarettes. These may kill you, but in the meantime they act as a calming influence on the user and an irritant to the opponent, especially if the butts are littered about the lawn. They are also a convenient indicator of wind direction.
Price: £2; value ☆☆☆.

Most musical, most melancholy

When I first wrote the music on the opposite page I was setting the words *"Tristitia et anxietas occupaverunt interiora mea; maestum factum est cor meum in dolore"* which translates as "Sorrow and anxiety have seized hold of me; my heart has become melancholy with grief." It was only afterwards that I realised that my subconscious mind had been setting other words, and after losing in the final of the Scottish Open I slowly became aware what they had been. Who else but a croquet player could feel the depth of emotion they convey? I know that before I took up croquet I could never have summoned up the despair necessary to express myself in this way.

If you wish to perform the work (necessarily *in camera*, I suspect, for it was designed as a chamber work), you may replace the viola da gamba parts by cellos or, if it is thought more appropriate, by kazoos. But the singer must have missed a short roquet in the previous four hours.

Ash Wednesday

Memento, homo, quia pulvis es.

While I feel a sombre, classical mood upon me, I am moved to tell you a true story of something that happened at the Edinburgh tournament, which takes place every year at Fettes College. The lawns are specially prepared for the tournament from the outfield of the first XI cricket pitch, and every morning the manager and his volunteers turn up early to set the hoops and put in the corner flags. On one occasion, after two days had successfully been completed, the manager was puzzled to find on his arrival a light covering of powder on one of the lawns, and being an agricultural gentleman tested it gingerly by taste and smell to see if it was some sort of bone-meal fertiliser, or possibly a weed-killer which had been applied the previous night. It smelt and tasted of nothing he could recognise and we proceeded to play over it.

The college groundsman arrived after a while, and the manager asked if he had any knowledge of the substance. "Och, aye," he said. "We scattered them there last nicht. Auld Erchie took sic guid care o' the cricket field that we kent there wis but ane place tae pit his ashes. Man, but it wis a braw still nicht yestere'en."

We took good care of Erchie's lawns that morning.

A croquet player's lament

DR Appleton 1993

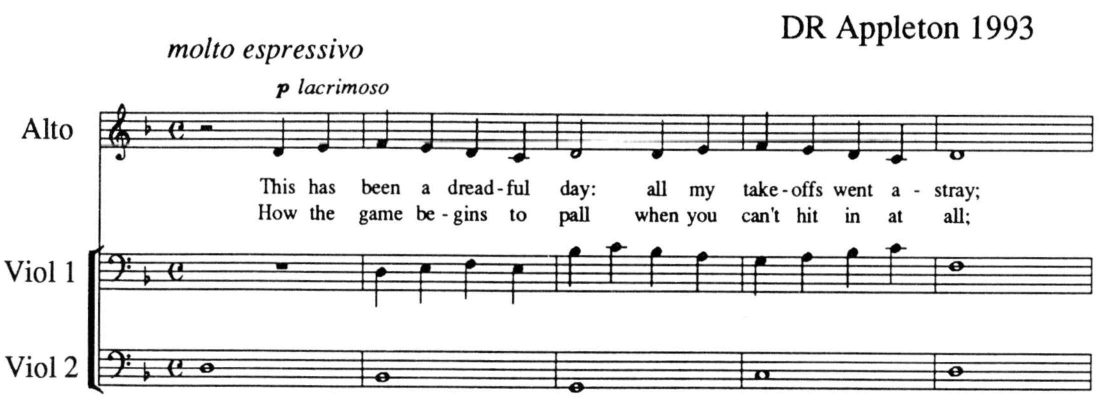

A Croquet Quiz

(answers on page 84)

1. After whom is the MacRobertson Shield named?

2. Which teams play for the Solomon Trophy?

3. What is the name of the trophy for the annual fixture between the CA and the SCA?

4. How many world champions have there been, and who is the only one who isn't English?

5. Where, and in which year, was croquet played at the Olympic Games?

6. Who has played most often for Scotland in the Home Internationals, and who is the only person (so far) to captain a winning Scottish side in them?

7. John Solomon won the English Open 9 times. Who won it 8 times, and who 7?

8. What is the connection between the photograph and the Scottish Open?

9. RDC, CHL and WdeB have all played for Wales. What is their surname, and which of them sometimes played under the alias Eamon Holiday?

10. Who holds the record for most wins in the Championship of Ireland, and whose record did he beat?

11. What did Lt Cdr RD Sinclair do in 1967, which was emulated by Bill Spalding, Dr RM Milne and Bob MacLean in the following three years?

12. Which New Zealand player is in the photograph, and what world record did he break in 1991-92?

13. Who won the Australian Open Championship for the first time in 1992, although he had previously won at Sonoma?

14. Who completed the first sextuple peel in America, and what nationality was he?

15. In which of the United States are Sonoma-Cutrer and Chattooga?

In principle I like the game, but there must be a way of speeding it up.

Alternative geometries

Here we play croquet for eternity. The balls are behind you.

A croquet crossword by Dis

(Solution on page 91.)

There are 6 kinds of clue.

Roquets are single clues, each to a four-letter word which travels parallel to a boundary and ends up in contact with a ball.

Hoop-running strokes are single clues to words which pass straight through the hoops.

Thick take-offs are clues to two words which begin in the same place and go at right angles to each other. The direction of each word must be deduced.

Split-shots are like take-offs, except the words go at 45° to each other.

Corner-cannons involve sending 3 words out from each corner, two along the boundaries, and one through the nearest hoop. (The flags are in the corners.)

Rolls are double clues to two 6-letter words which begin in adjacent squares and travel parallel to each other; either word may be clued first. All the letter pairs they form are words (always taking the same word first), e.g.

```
ESKIMO
MOANER
```

The double-bankers are on the lawn, and the end of the game should be obvious.

The Chambers Dictionary (1993) is recommended.

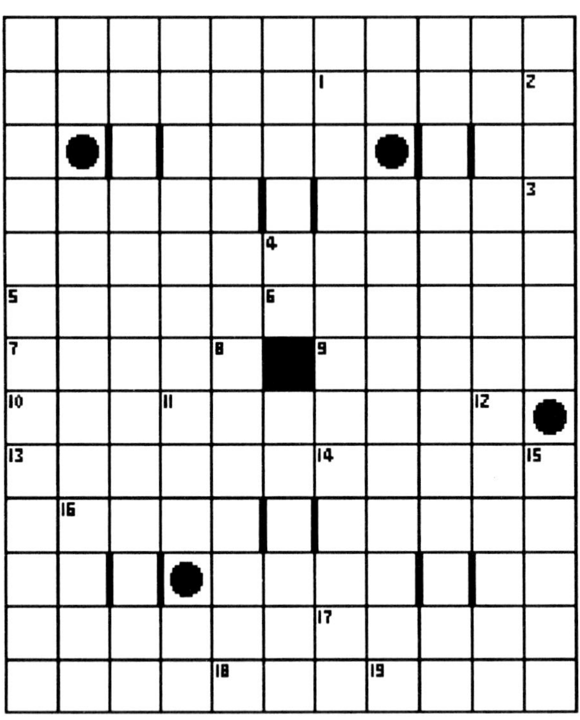

Roquets

Rotten, rotten to shed tear.
Scottish bear is seen returning in sheer dismay.
This Russian prince would be strong with you French around.
Yes, a scattering is convenient.

Hoop-running strokes

Hoop 1 Guard take in a bundle of banknotes. (4)
Hoop 2 Rand is in a mess; change to gold coins. (6)
Hoop 3 Large quantities, sometimes falling on people. (4)
Hoop 4 Brother William's leader in part of mine ... (4)
Hoop 5 ... therefore monster is rejected. (4)
Hoop 6 Union St ahead; there *would* be a blockage. (6)

1-back Queen executed one. (4)
2-back Glanced, attracted, taken out. (5)
3-back Venus is in this golden girl. (5)
4-back Ancient piece, not quite a gold coin. (6)
Penultimate Native woman's cape without tie-on label. (3)
Rover Inexperienced environmentalist. (5)

Thick take-offs

2. Country lover (not Irishman) gives a striking display. (4)
   To do this is part of Isis' prowess. (3)
7. The Women's Institute's turned pale. (5)
   Clean a seat back to front. (4)
9. Fantastic complicated route. (5)
   Scottish grandchild holds record in science. (5)
11. Fed up with employment? Do what the bomb squad does. (6)
    Look! An overdose will bring about grief. (4)
14. It might burn with rage after golf shot. (3,4)
    Allows hindrances. (4)
17. Little book, little brook, flat fish (5)
    Bubble (cry) for half an hour. (4)

Split shots

1. Poseur'd make _____ or ... (5)
   ... slightly socialistic small Shakespearian. (4)
3. Discreet Scottish guide. (4)
   Women love all long thick curly hair. (4)
5. Grieve for Henry I. (4)
   Light upon odd material in hoist. (3)
7. It could be a piece of cake, for example, to be able to go back. (5)
   Poteen loses its heart and becomes watery stuff. (4)
8. Ornamental stone head lost in street. (4)
   That's little George in the gully. (3)
8. Beyond help; grounded, with every other character superfluous ... (4)
   ... or yellow. (4)
12. Pub one rejected; one is on wagon. (5)
    Help leaders of Africa improve democracy. (3)
15. Shake particle off a large cube. (5)
    Is it a root? Partly. (4)
16. Dreadful. King is in hazard. (4)
    Pulse, one from face. (3)
18. Lead astray after midnight in a spot in the woods. (5)
    Edmonds' first leg slip catch. (4)
19. Crazy London deb has two heads; this one ... (6)
    ... and The Duke's Head? (3)

Corner-cannons

I. Drunken binge around noon. Gracious! (6)
   Pound: clever in parts. (4)
   Black music's pride. (4)
II. Short second tries after failure? (6)
    Pan actors, miscast and missing leader of company. (5)
    Doe's opponent, or perhaps doe. (3)
III. A learner in detonation produces broken stone. (7)
     British possess a lot of game birds. (5)
     Mouthful which sounds only part of a word. (4)
IV. Move unsteadily before gin cocktail with touch of nepenthe in it makes one drowsy. (7)
    Torn entry forms: torn long ago. (5)
    Turn over squirrel's nest in garden. (4)

Rolls

4 & 6. Fancy! In the middle of the day Italian lies back fast asleep. Pass silently.
10 & 13. It's displeasing, missing on the right, going less than a foot dead beside two balls. Bad luck.

Miss Marple and the 1-back leave

A short story by Dorothy Rush

'When the gods play croquet, they undoubtedly use 1b tactics.'
Keith Wylie

I do not remember whether Agatha Christie ever mentioned that Jane Marple was a croquet player, but she most certainly must have been: croquet would have been just her game. In fact I am sure that I glimpsed her on lawn five at Cheltenham one day last year, but of course that might well have been one of several other worthy ladies.

Here then, with apologies to the beloved memory of both Miss Christie and Miss Marple, is the story that the one might have written about the other.

The rectory at St Mary Mead rejoices in one of the finest croquet lawns in England, and England is a land where the nurture of stretches of level greensward has so preoccupied the inhabitants that they have invented or adopted as their national sports, games which involve not so much the playing of sport upon grass, as the watching of grass upon which these sports are being played. It is not the activities themselves which matter but the velvety greenness of their setting. Hence, the Englishman sits at a cricket match with no more than a cursory glance at the play, and in croquet the matter is even further advanced, for here no-one, not even the outplayer, pays the game any attention at all, but luxuriates instead in the proximity of all that lovely, flat grass.

But it is the lawn of St Mary Mead's rectory that we are considering, and on a warm day in late summer a small group of somewhat ill-assorted people were gathered along the north boundary. This boundary, I should mention, runs precisely west to east, a fact which indicates that the construction of this impeccable lawn was no fortuitous accident but the result of a deal of careful planning. Five of those present, keen croquet players all, were aware of this; the other two were humble, though large members of the local police force who knew nothing of such esoteric matters and indeed would have blithely perambulated their size twelves all over the hallowed turf, had not the Rector himself prevailed upon them to desist.

"We shall 'ave to go onto the lawn eventually sir, to inspect and remove the body," Sergeant Courtney spoke in measured and patient tones. "Unless you'ld like us to 'over above the spot, sir." He allowed himself a small smile: "Unfortunately sir, as you doubtless appreciate, pigs can't fly!"

"That joke is in very bad taste, Sergeant, and not at all in keeping with the sadness of the occasion. Mr Fellows was not only a respected and much-loved member of our close-knit village community, he was also a minus player and tipped for the President's

Cup this year. We shall miss him profoundly, and I hope you are going to bring his killer to book forthwith.

The Reverend Doctor Bender was beginning to lose his habitual calm.

"Well sir, I can't solve the crime, if such it be, till I've made a close examination of the victim, and ascertained the circumstances in which he died, now can I sir? So 'ow about you letting me and Constable Boswell 'ere approach the corpse in the manner laid down in regulations, eh?" He spoke gently as to a small child. Gesturing to his colleague, he was about to pulverise the sacred turf when a tiny but firm and restraining hand grasped his arm. He looked down with a sigh at the frail figure of an old lady whom he knew well as one of those village busy-bodies who appear, like moths around the police-station lamp, whenever a whiff of scandal is in the air.

"Well, Miss Marple, what is it now?" The sergeant's patience began to wear a little thin.

"If I may, Sergeant, I should like to prevail upon you to respect what I know would have been the wishes of the deceased in this matter. Had he known he was going to be murdered, he would have gone to any lengths to see that no harm would be caused to the lawn, either in the committing of the crime or in the solving of it. It puts me in mind of dear Virginia Braithwaite who used to live at Stretton Magna: when she decided to commit suicide by jumping out of a chestnut tree onto her own tennis courts she was very careful to land on the en-tout-cas and not on the grass court.

"No, Sergeant, there are some things a dedicated player will not do, and dying violently in the vicinity of the sixth hoop is one that Brian Fellows would have tried very hard to avoid."

"Now look 'ere, madam, I've got my job to do, and do it I must, in spite of your misplaced desire to protect the grass. The cause of death must be ascertained without further delay."

"I should have thought *that* at least was obvious, old bean," drawled a young man in white shorts and tennis shoes, who was leaning nonchalantly on a slim-shafted croquet mallet. Presumably that corner-flag sticking out from between his shoulder-blades had something to do with it."

His companion, a blonde girl with big baby-blue eyes, who clung possessively to his arm, giggled, drawing a frown from the Rector.

"May I ask your name sir?" said Constable Boswell ponderously, taking out his notebook and a newly sharpened pencil.

"You may indeed, old thing. It's Hargreaves, Ronnie to my friends, and one or two other things to this gorgeous creature at my side, whose name is Cynthia — or to you, Miss Boundford. Cynthia, say hello to the nice policeman."

Cynthia giggled again. "Hello, nice policeman," she said seductively.

Miss Marple had been witnessing this exchange with clear disapproval. "I really think you ought not to speak to the officer like that, Ronald."

"Sorry, Aunt Jane, just nervous tension really. I was pretty fond of old Brian, even if he did beat me hollow every time we played."

Miss Marple continued to hold the sergeant's sleeve in apparent absent-mindedness. "There really is no need, you know, to go onto the lawn in order to deduce exactly what happened."

While the long-suffering policeman stands in open-mouthed amazement at this astonishing statement, let us consider the most important protagonist of this tale — the one without whom, as it were, none of this would have been possible. I refer of course to the victim, the late Mr Brian Fellows.

He had been found, a short while before, by the handsome young twosome, Ronnie and Cynthia, as they came onto the lawn for an early-morning game. The Rector not only allowed the village's group of keen croqueteers to play on his lawn, he encouraged them to practise as often as they could, for it was his dearest wish to lead a team to victory in the Croquet Association's Interclub competition. Brian Fellows had been the shining hope of his ambitious plans.

So there they had found the minus player's cold body, stretched as though asleep on that delicious turf, his head resting on his left arm, and in his right hand his favourite Solomon mallet, his right arm stretched out towards the sixth hoop and his feet pointing towards hoop two. When the young people had fetched the Rector and his friend Miss Marple, who had just happened to drop in for rather early elevenses, the face of the dead croqueteer had been found to be bathed incongruously in a broad and satisfied smile.

A call to the local police station had brought the boys in blue at a trot, eager to solve this crime before Miss Marple could interfere yet again. (It is a curious fact, worthy of notice here, that for a small village St Mary Mead had an astonishing crime rate. In spite of this, however, the local bobbies were hard put to get any practice at solving these crimes due to the activities of the ubiquitous Miss Marple, who kept popping up with the solution before the forces of law could get their act together. Hence the speed with which Messrs Courtney and Boswell had arrived on the scene.)

Thus it was with ill-disguised irritation that the good sergeant bent his gaze once more to the small figure of Jane Marple in her flowered summer frock and, finally, managed to stammer a few words: "I 'ave a nasty feeling, Miss Marple, that I don't want to 'ear this, but I'll ask anyway: 'ow on hearth do you know what 'appened?"

Miss Marple smiled in kindly fashion and released the policeman's arm. "Perhaps we could all sit down if Jennings would be so good as to bring out the folding chairs."

She turned to the middle-aged man who had, until this moment, remained standing in silence on the fringe of the group, a faintly cynical grin on his weatherbeaten features, and a bright-eyed sheepdog at his side. This was the gardener, Jennings, whose skill had created and now tended one of the finest lawns in England. He bestirred himself now, and set out six chairs, choosing his own seat on the stump of an old elm.

When all were seated, Miss Marple looked around rather smugly. "The crime," she said, "which has been committed here is not punishable by your law, Sergeant Courtney, but what will be immediately clear to my dear friends here as I unravel the mystery, is that Brian Fellows died because he was a minus player, and not just an ordinary minus player but a minus 3. That was the reason for his tragic demise."

"Look here, Aunt Jane, I'm sorry but I can't see why a chap has to die for being a minus player, even a minus three. I'm a scratch player myself and hope to go down another half soon. Shall I expect to be murdered shortly?"

"Be patient dear, and all will be revealed. What you must remember is that minus players — and especially minus 3s — never, ever practise. I believe I am right in saying that the famous Mr Wylie did not practise for ten years. So what do they do instead? No, Cynthia, that was a rhetorical question, and I intend to answer it myself. Instead of practising, dear friends and gentlemen of the police, they play croquet with the gods. Never seen on the lawns by day, at night they set the hoops to a 1/64" clearance, open a new set of Jaques balls (second colours, of course, to avoid those over-sized blacks) and play game after game against celestial opponents and by the ethereal light of the stars.

"Which is precisely what Brian was doing last night when he was, perhaps inevitably, killed. When Ronald and Cynthia found him, he had been lying there since a little after midnight."

"How can you possibly know the time of death without recourse to the medical evidence?" asked the constable, who was studying for his sergeant's exams.

"I shall make that very clear before I'm finished, Constable, if you can just manage to be patient. First I should like to explain how I am certain that Brian's opponent in this, his final match, was a godly croquet player: if you examine the position of the balls and clips, you will see that white and pink are cross-wired at the first hoop, green is in the jaws of 1-back, and brown about a yard north of that hoop. All the clips bar the green are on the crown of the first hoop, the green clip being on the side of 1-back. Any croquet player, Sergeant, certainly any minus player, would know that this is the 1-back leave. Now, Mr Wylie informs us, in his excellent treatise on the game, that when the gods play croquet, they undoubtedly use 1-back tactics, and this is how I know, not only that Brian Fellows was playing against a member of that heavenly croquet club, but also that his opponent hit the fourth shot and, having made hoop 6, left what he thought was a perfect 1-back leave.

"Unfortunately, Brian was a minus 3 and minus 3s never miss a trick. He spotted that not only were white and pink wired from each other, and of course green, but brown was fractionally too close to hoop 2 to give a clear shot to the pink. Brian believed that he had a lift, and had turned with his mallet raised to call a referee. Hence the reversed grip of his hand on the mallet (Brian always used a Solomon grip for his shots), and the curious position of his arm above his head, even as he lies there."

Miss Marple paused a moment, looking at each of her listeners in turn. "And hence, I would say, the extraordinary smile of triumph on poor Brian's face. He thought that he was about to perform the first sextuple peel on the opponent in the universe — on one of the gods, no less — and possibly be reduced to minus 3 and a half!"

"Well, that's most interesting, Jane, but it does not explain, to me at least, why he's lying there dead on my lawn." Once more Dr Bender was showing clear signs of profound agitation.

"If I may be allowed to borrow the expression,

it's elementary, my dear Rector. Brian's opponent, enraged at the insult to his august person, caused the red flag to rise from the ground and imbed itself violently between Brian's poor mortal shoulder-blades, killing him instantly."

Sergeant Courtney rose to his feet. "Well that settles it for me, Miss Marple. Looks like you've done it again. I expect the Super'll be wanting to 'ave a word with you later, but for now I'll just go gack to the station and write up my report. Come along Boswell."

The young policeman hesitated. "Just one more thing, Miss Marple. You haven't explained how you knew that the death occurred at midnight."

"A little after twelve, to be exact," said Miss Marple primly, "and that was the easy part. Last night I happened to be awake rather late, writing to my dear friend Jessica, who's gone to Budleigh Salterton for the sea-air. A few minutes after midnight there was a sudden and terrific gust of wind which shook the house but passed almost immediately. This I take to be the gust of wind with which Brian's opponent propelled his improvised dart. Moreover, on the way here this morning I noticed that the weather vane from the roof of the village hall had been torn from its elevated position, and hurled in an east-south-easterly direction across the village green to imbed itself in the church clock, stopping it at precisely 3 minutes past 12. East-south-east is, of course, the direction in which the red flag must have flown to hit Brian as he walked towards hoop 6.

"But at least he died happy, knowing that he had the game in his pocket."

Miss Marple stopped speaking and began to gather up her handbag, parasol and cardigan. The two policemen walked briskly towards their car, shaking their heads as they exchanged comments of evident amazement and bravely disguised disgruntlement.

The Rector took Jane Marple's arm as they returned with the two young people to the house. The body of Brian Fellows, who, but for the intervention of the gods, might have seen his handicap fall to -3½, lay still upon the lawn, waiting to be removed by suitably shod undertakers.

Of the living, only Jennings the gardener remained, sitting on the stump of elm, his hand resting on the quiet sheepdog. He leaned down to speak to her confidingly as though she understood every word. "Silly old bat! She 'asn't been right in the 'ead since 'er friend Miss Christie died. It's me as stuck that corner-flag in his back, weren't it, my beauty? Practising his damned jump shots on my lawn and grinning like an idiot when I told 'im off. He deserved to die, didn't 'e? Bleedin' minus player!

So I said to the greenkeeper, "You're not indispensable, you know."

Croquet epitaphs

Sport's most famous epitaph is probably the one placed by English cricket supporters, which gave rise to the Ashes. Though croquet is very much alive and well the following may amuse. The first rather depends on an awareness that a) being on 4-back and 1-back (the two 'lift hoops') is sometimes known as 'having the clips of death', and b) Keith Wylie in his book *Expert Croquet Tactics* represents Blue and Black by the letters U and K respectively; in other books, for example *Croquet: The Skills of the Game* by Bill Lamb, the player of Red and Yellow is conventionally known as Ray, while his opponent is Bab. The rumours of Mrs Rush's demise are, thankfully, premature and she has graciously contributed articles of her own to this book.

The clips of death

Here lies a -2,
Pegged out while peeling K with U.
He just failed to come back
From 4-B & 1-B.

A crush Shot

Dolly Rush, alas, is dead:
A mallet struck her on the head.
She acted as a referee
When all the others were at tea.
They should have told her not to view
So carefully the follow-through.

The double-bankers

Under this slab
Lie Ray and Bab;
They wouldn't be seen
Playing Brown and Green.

A non-standard leave

Dead from a bite on his derrière,
Ian* was savaged by a pit-bull terrier;
Dogged by misfortune, his turn is over —
Stuck for ever in the jaws of Rover.

* A name chosen completely at random

Mind you, having our own croquet lawn did mean we had to forgo some other luxuries.

Intermediate gadgetry

Creating GOSSIP

In normal club use it is easy for balls from different sets to become mixed up. Practice and coaching in particular are likely to lead to the need for reassigning balls into sets, and it is often quite hard to reconstitute the original sets accurately. The most important thing is that balls in a set should have had comparable use and be close to the same size. Visual inspection should manage the first of these reasonably well, though I may not be alone in thinking that different colours of balls of the same make can show different patterns of wear.

What we are going to make in this article is a ball grader (or a Gravity Operated Sphere-Sorting Inclined Plane). It is possible to calibrate it accurately to size balls, but we have a more limited aim, which is just to sort balls in order of their size. A hardwood is easiest to work with; assuming your local DIY store is pretending to have gone metric, get a 2.4m length of 100mm by 19mm. You could use a 900mm by 300mm piece of Contiboard, but you have to be very accurate as you cannot smooth the joins off afterwards. The version on page 93 is in simulated black ash.

Start by sawing your wood into sections as shown in the plans on the next page. The lengths of the base and sides may be changed within reason, but the tapered piece which is to be the base must be cut with some precision, as must the two ends. You can saw the base to shape, but it is probably better to plane it. The pieces may conveniently be glued and screwed together, and a countersink which drills the two pieces of wood at the same time is useful. Make sure that the screws pass cleanly into the base through the sides and ends. Attach the bottom end to the sides first, then the base, and finally the top end.

Sit the assembled box on a level surface and let a ball roll down the inclined plane. Unless it is seriously too large or too small it should come to a stop somewhere between 50% and 80% of the way down. Determine the range for a large number of balls of all makes and divide this range, or a little more, into 10 or 12 equal intervals by marking the base or the tops of the sides. You can then give a score to each ball and arrange your sets appropriately. By repeatedly rolling an individual ball you can determine how variable is the distance it descends, and this will give you a measurement of how spherical it is.

GOSSIP with your friends about what you have made; they are sure to be impressed. You may even be able to turn this device into a money-spinning game of chance for winter evenings at your club. Take a ball of a well-known make and accept bets on where it will stop when released down the slope.

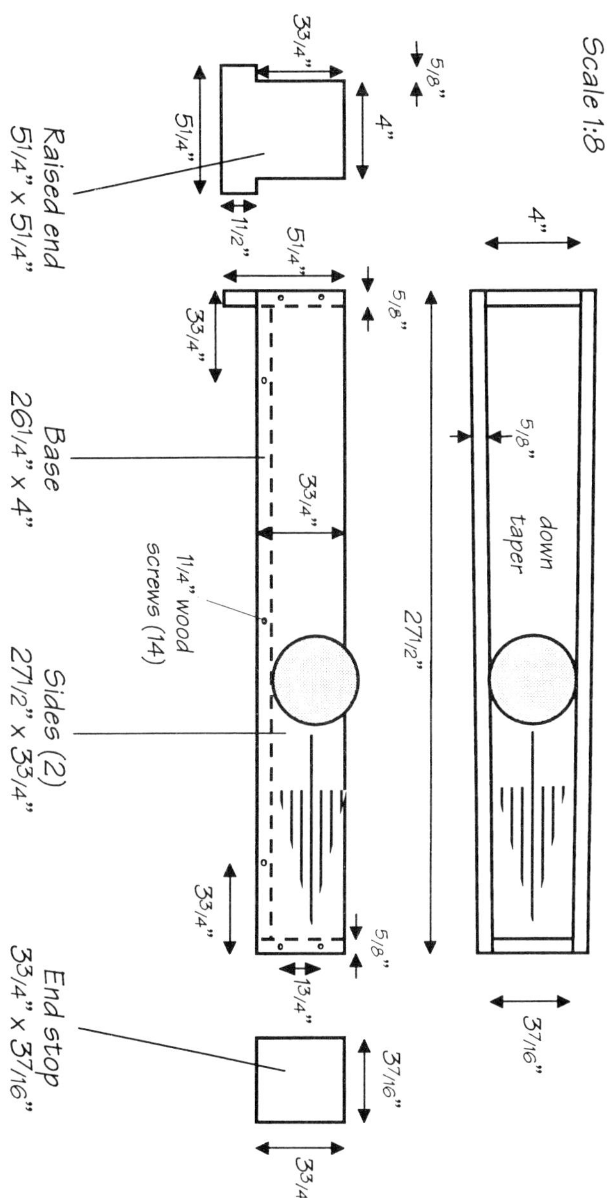

A different angle on things

If you place a ball 9" in front of hoop 6, and then stand over the flag in corner I, the angle between the south boundary and the centre of the ball is almost exactly 60°. (That information is more useful than you might think!)

Could I just have a word with you about that last bisque you took to peg out?

Taking the bisque

No, ladies... I'm all for initiative, but that is not the intended way to use bisques.

You're right. It's not the normal way to use a bisque, but it's very effective.

A Croquet Dream

(experienced while waiting
for a visiting team to arrive)

Towards the court she glides to stalk her ball.
A slender figure, elegant and tall,
She makes the roquet, and with easy grace
Each ball is sent to its appointed place.
A rush towards her hoop is smoothly made;
A little split approach is gently played;
And then, with body and with head so still,
She makes the hoop with conscious act of will.
Of confidence and skill she has her share;
Her swing is straight; her game is full of flair;
Not short of strength to play a big pass-roll,
Yet has the touch to run hoops with control.
She knows just where it's best each ball should go;
She plays with care, but never gets too slow.
Her shots are sure, her nerves are made of steel --
She's almost bound to get this triple peel.
Another hoop succumbs -- a super break
With not the slightest hint of a mistake.
She only has the rover peel to do,
And then she'll make penultimate off blue.
That's nicely done, the end is almost near;
It looks as though she'll win the cup this year.
But what's she done? That's not the shot to play!
I think she'll find that trouble lies that way.
One stroke has just destroyed her purple patch.
It's my turn now, and I can win this match.

It's a funny old game

Perhaps it is because too many croquet players are trained in the more scientific disciplines, such as computing and chemistry, mathematics and metallurgy, that no proper attention has been given to the origins of the game. Prichard's otherwise excellent *The History of Croquet* would have us believe that the game originated, probably in Ireland, in the 19th century; I hope to show that it was already popular in the England of the first Elizabeth, and indeed that Shakespeare himself was a thoughtful, enthusiastic, though possibly not a particularly consistent player. He was almost certainly a qualified referee.

It would be wrong, however, to extrapolate from references in *Macbeth* and *Julius Caesar* to the assumption that croquet was played in mediaeval Scotland or classical Rome. Shakespeare wrote of other times, but for his own time from his own experience, and the references were intended to be understood and taken to heart by his own audiences.

We can see how he gained their sympathy, as he still gains ours, for King Duncan who *will plead ... against the damnation of his taking off*; do we not all feel like that when the croqueted ball doesn't move, when it is *unshak'd of motion* as Caesar puts it? Have we not all cried out with Mark Antony that *this was the most unkindest cut of all*, and cursed with Macbeth *the devil damn thee black*? We must all feel for Othello who did *speak of some distressful stroke*, and during the close season we agonise with King Lear who could only *hear poor rogues talk of court news*.

This was the most unkindest cut of all

Not all the references are as easy to interpret: are the witches bemoaning leaving a double target, or is Shakespeare through them cautioning against putting a four-ball break in peril by attempting a double peel in the incantation *double, double toil and trouble*? It is because of the depth of feeling in these quotations — notice that they all come from tragedies — that I suggest that their author probably played off no better than about 6 bisques, but it may be that in 1599 and 1605, when he wrote *Julius Caesar* and *Macbeth*, that he was rather off his game.

Double, double toil and trouble

In the comedies and the sonnets he is generally much more positive and offers some advice on tactics. In *A Midsummer Night's Dream* Bottom says he *could play ... to make all split* (a good season in 1595?), and in the sonnets — were WH and the dark lady regular doubles partners? — he discusses the leave (*when yellow leaves*) and points out how early in the break it must be planned: *thou must leave ere long*. In Henry VIII, written in 1612 by which time he was very experienced, he criticises a high-bisquer who *puts forth the tender leave of hope*. There are ambiguities in the sonnets too: is *all men make faults* a cry of anguish about himself (another poor season in 1594 perhaps), or was he starting his interest in refereeing?

This last pervades the plays: Hamlet, possibly hoopbound, calls for a referee who awards a roquet: *a hit, a very palpable hit*; Cassius very correctly has *all his faults observed*, and Caesar himself is heavily penalised, possibly for persistent double-tapping for *it was a grievous fault, and grievously hath Caesar answered it*. By 1603, in Measure for Measure, Shakespeare's refereeing was so skilled that *every fault's condemned ere it be done.*

Apart from the advice on the leave, Shakespeare offers two other coaching hints. On hoop-running he recommends (in *King Lear*) that one should *strike flat the thick rotundity* and declares (in *Merchant of Venice*): *I will not jump with common spirits.* Clearly there was a tendency among his contemporaries to try to force the ball through, but he favoured a smooth stroke to run the hoop with control.

What sort of playing conditions the Elizabethans had for croquet is difficult to determine: Shakespeare's only reference is

A hit, a very palpable hit

to a *lawn as white as driven snow*, but that is from *The Winter's Tale*. From other available sources — the *Prayer Book* (1662) and the *King James Bible* (1611) — we hear that *the grass withereth* and *my soul hath a desire to enter in to the courts of the Lord ... for one day in Thy courts is better than a thousand.* This might indicate poor lawns, but perhaps one should only draw such a conclusion about the vicarage gardens of the day.

There is much further research for the historian to do in these books, and in the works of other authors. Who was the player of whom it was said that his *driving is like the driving of Jehu ... for he driveth furiously*? And how much was the *Prayer Book* a manual of croquet etiquette: *I acknowledge my faults*? What of Marlowe's difficulty in getting the balls to remain in contact for a croquet stroke: *stand still you ever-moving spheres*, and Bacon's advice on taking bisques: *a man must make his opportunity as oft as find it*? But whatever exegetics may offer in the future, it will be impossible to come to any conclusion other than that in the first Elizabethan age, as in the second, people of learning and culture spent their leisure playing croquet.

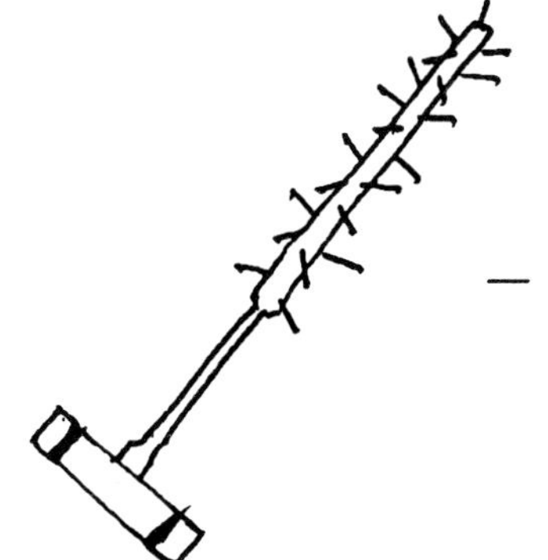

The Fakir

A favourite of Indian players. Unlikely to be used by other players in error.

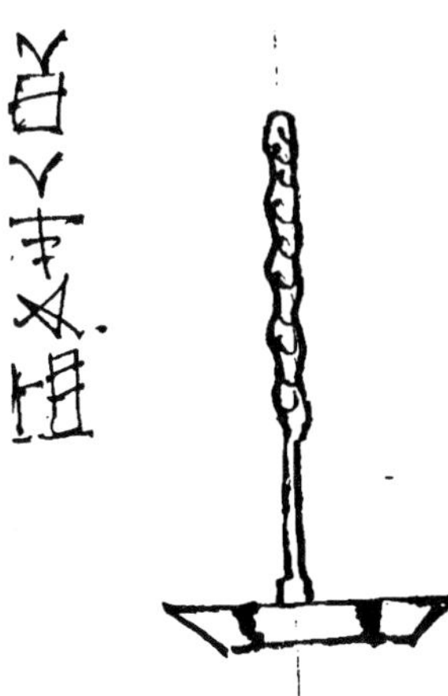

The Missan

A Japanese design, to be used when playing the boss. Guarantees a topped ball at every stroke.

The Falstaff

for the overweight player. Swivel head prevents undue wear.

More

The Crutch

Useful for those players who spend most of their matches waiting to get the innings.

The Aquahead

Designed for playing on flooded lawns. Hollow head minimises water resistance when striking submerged ball.

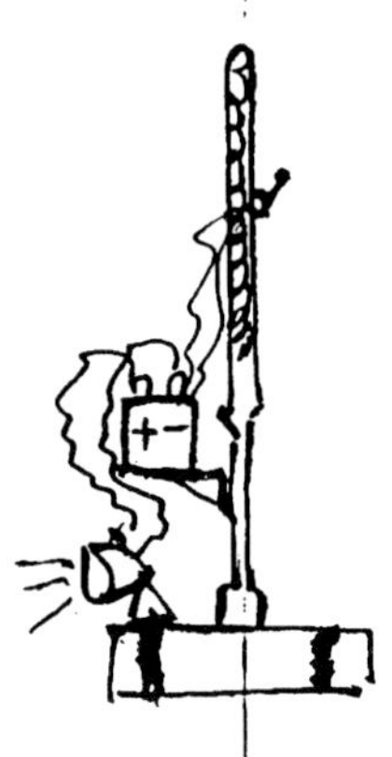

The Nightrider

A flick of the switch gives you the edge in that late evening match.

Mallets

The Bandit

Designed for coaches who teach beginners. Guarantees fast results for the ambitious club.

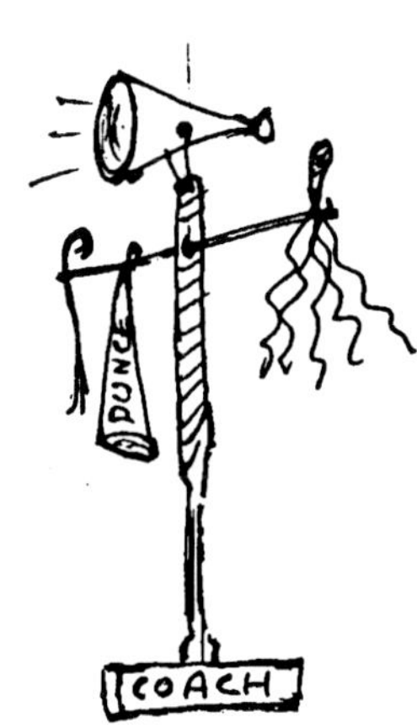

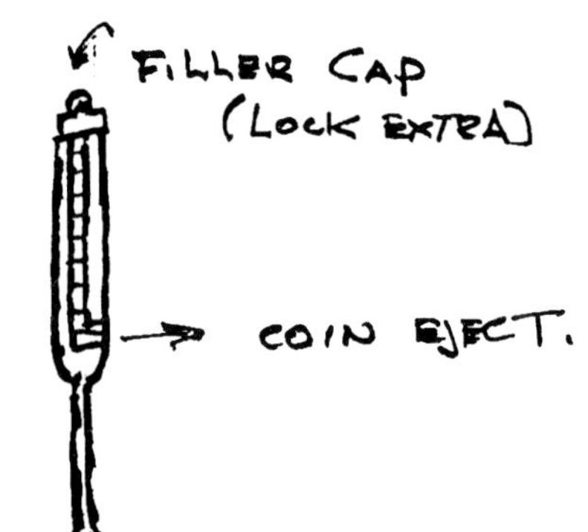

The Marker

You'll never be looking for a marker with this coin-holding mallet. Takes 1p, 2p & 5p coins.

It's your shot, partner

As soon as questions of will or decision or reason or choice of action arise, human science is at a loss.

Noam Chomsky

Things and actions are what they are, and the consequences of them will be what they will be ... but to us probability is the very guide of life.

Bishop Butler

Now then, partner! You are playing with Black and are for the peg. Blue (that's me) has been pegged out by Yellow, which has given Red, for rover, a good rush to its hoop from the south boundary a couple of yards west of hoop 1. You are in the middle of the east boundary, from where you can see Red and Yellow (Fig 1). It is you to play. All the bisques are gone and there is still half an hour till 'time'. (Thank goodness for that; this is going to get complicated enough!) I'll tell you what you should do.

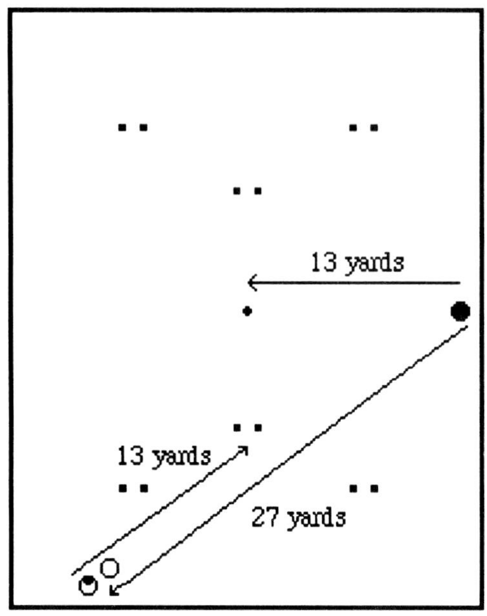

Fig 1

Don't panic! we could still win the Club Doubles Championship. But should you shoot at the peg, or at Red and Yellow, or should you trickle to the peg? Just a minute; let's think about it. We both have a pretty good idea of your capabilities (well I have: you rather tend to overestimate them), but let us keep them vague for the moment: we shall suppose that you have probability p_1 of hitting the peg by shooting across the court (ie that p_1 is the proportion of times you will succeed). Maybe p_1 will be about 0.2, so that on average you will hit the peg once in five such shots. Some rough calculations show that your probability of hitting a ball 27 or 28 yards away is about two-thirds of the probability of hitting the peg from 13 yards. The probability of hitting a double target (Red and Yellow exactly a ball's width apart) at the distance shown in Fig 1 is therefore about $4p_1/3$. Your third option is to trickle to the peg: let us assume that you have probability p_2 of actually hitting it (one chance in 20?), and that you are absolutely certain of getting close enough to peg out next time, if you get a shot from there: I suppose I can rely on you to do that? While we are making these assumptions we might as well suppose that your nerves are strong enough to effect a peg-out if you hit Red or Yellow, or to make a short roquet should your opponent leave you one, for example by clanging rover off your ball at some stage. Well, what more do you need to know? Get on with it. Don't keep our opponents waiting.

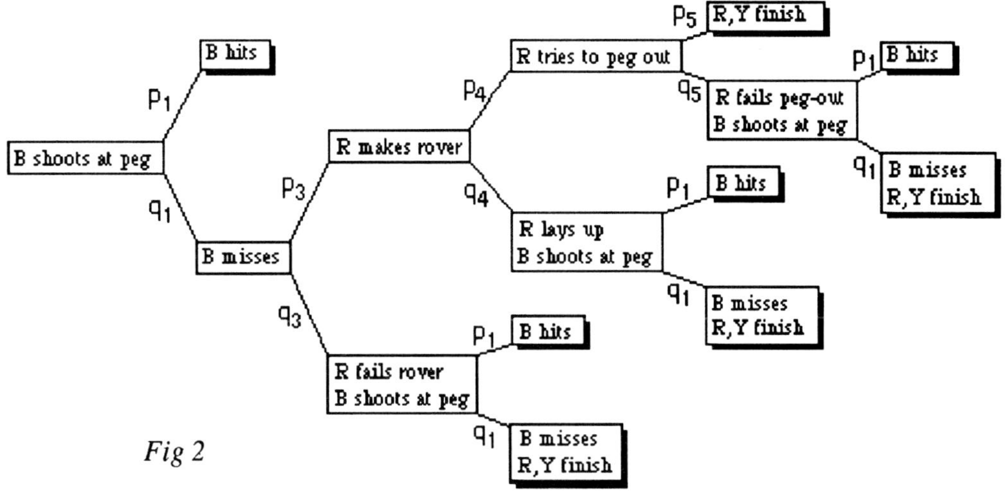

Fig 2

What? Oh, yes. I suppose we do have to consider our opponent's ability. How likely is he to make rover if you leave him his rush? Will he peg out if he runs it? Will he try to use your ball if you leave it by the peg? We shall have to make a few more assumptions. Suppose (without it being in any way a negative thought) that you shoot at the peg and miss. He will make rover with probability p_3. If he is successful he may try to peg out (say with probability p_4) or he may lay up . If he goes for the peg out he will succeed with probability p_5. Of course he may succeed with one ball and fail with the other. (I told you it would get complicated; it's just as well there aren't four balls on the lawn.) What might the values for these new probabilities be? Shall we say 0.9 for p_3, 0.8 for p_4, and 0.7 for p_5? And to make it easy, let's conveniently forget about him pegging out one ball, but we'll suppose that if he chooses to lay up or if he misses the peg-out he will finish next time unless you hit the peg.

Let's not consider the other options yet, but look at the possibilities so far. (See I've drawn you a decision tree.) Oh dear, I have slipped in another assumption: if Red fails to make rover and you still don't hit the peg he finishes. I know it might not be true, but since the chances are very good that he will make rover anyway, it's not going to affect the situation very much, and it really is time you were back on the lawn. At least we now know that the probability of winning if you shoot at the peg is

$$p_1\{1+(1-p_1)(1-p_3p_4p_5)\}$$

and for the values we have been using that comes to 0.28. No, partner, you are not allowed to evaluate the expression with used bisques; law 49c, you know.

Looks like we're not in with too good a chance that way. Let's see what happens if we shoot at them or trickle to the peg. Just let me sharpen my pencil.

I say, partner, where are you? Don't take your shot yet; I haven't worked out all the probabilities. What are you doing? You only have a 0.28 chance of winning if you do that.

Oh, good shot partner! I always knew we could do it!

Classical Jack

Pharaoh seems to think your mind hasn't been on your work these last few weeks.

Dr Livingstone, I presume?

Rodin's "Mixed-doubles winners"

Will they get a surprise!

Run rover

This vicious little puzzle was contributed by Syd Jones, who, several years ago, constructed a version of it in plastic. What is shown as a large circle is a croquet ball, and the two small circles are a hoop. The rectangles edged in black can slide around, because there is a gap represented by the shaded area. The object is to move the rectangles so that the ball passes through the hoop; no other pieces must pass through it, of course. I am grateful to Syd for refusing to give me the solution and forcing me finally to solve the puzzle so that I could include it here. (My solution is on page 88.)

A short croquet crossword by Dis

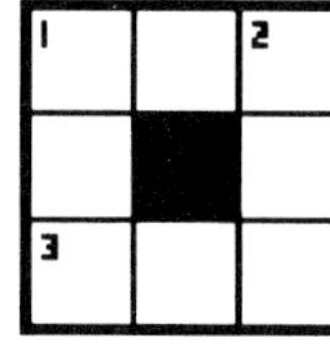

1 *ac.* Idle learner goes off – idiot!
3 *ac.* Easy take-off from here?
1 *dn.* Amusing blunder knocks her out. Could she give two hoots?
2 *dn.* Shot to settle dilemma.

Alice's illustrated guide

The Croquet Association has published an etiquette guide. Some of its precepts are illustrated here with a little help from Sir John Tenniel and a versifier of rather more moderate talent.

Such tips should help novices at tournaments avoid the strictures of experienced players, though they should be aware that the sentence of the Queen of Hearts (mere execution) is regarded by some as rather mild for a high bisquer who ventures, in violation of sacred convention, to toss up at the start of a game.

"Some players do not welcome remarks during the course of a game."

Your opponent is rather reserved;
His silence has got you unnerved.
Well, don't lose your cool
And chat like a fool.
The proprieties must be observed.

to croquet etiquette

If you must have an hour or so free,
Ask the manager when it should be,
Lest his plans you should shatter,
Make him mad as a hatter,
And he won't give you time off for tea.

"Do not take a meal without confirming with the manager."

When you've played through your game at a crawl,
And it's 'time' by the referee's call,
Since you should have a watch
To time your own match,
It shouldn't surprise you at all.

"Carry a watch."

If you lose a game, be of good cheer:
Your opponent will buy you a beer.
But don't have a short
If you're straight back on court;
The effects can be really quite queer.

"The winner usually buys the drinks after the game (if appropriate)."

Coaching tips #3

The New Standard Leave

The first two of these coaching tips were on leaves, and so is this one. Why? Because it is through your leaves that you attempt to control the shape of a game: to make it go at the speed and with the grace (or dourness) you want it to. The crosswire can be attempted by any reasonable player against an equal or lower-bisqued player, perhaps in the latter case with the aid of a bisque to tidy it up; leaving the balls in the corners is the prerogative of the expert in a handicap match when there are bisques remaining against him. The new standard leave (NSL) is a good one for B-class players who are keen to try for a triple peel in a game played under the rules for 'advanced' play. The first triple I achieved from a leave (rather than an opponent breaking down) was certainly from an NSL.

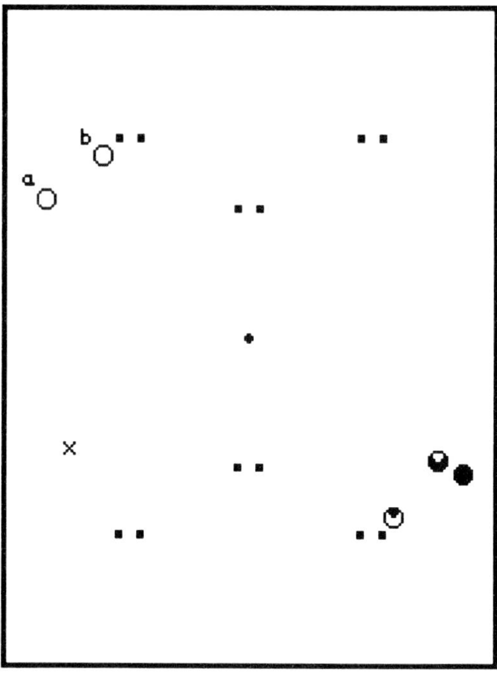

There are really two versions of the leave, depending where the ball near hoop 2 is left. Let us suppose that the player with the innings is playing with blue and has chosen to leave yellow near hoop 2. It may be in either of the positions shown in the diagram, and we shall come back to the reasons for its position later. Of course, if both opponent balls are for hoop one, it does not matter whether yellow or red is left at the second hoop, but if yellow were for one and red for 2 it would be very foolish to leave yellow there. If yellow is for one and red for 4-back, leaving yellow at two is certainly inviting your opponent to lift it, hit black and finish with a triple. In other words this is a leave which gives you a good chance of a triple, but it can offer your opponent a very easy break if he hits.

More of that later: what we are really concerned with is how to get the balls into the correct positions. As usual you must plan ahead, but not too much: it is helpful if you can put black in as an early pioneer at 2-back, make 6 off red and 1-back off yellow. However only a little ingenuity is necessary after hoop 5 to convert the other five combinations of red, yellow and black as pivot and pioneers for hoops 5 and 6 into an NSL. Once you can do it the easy way you can experiment at leisure.

Having run hoop 6, rush the red across to 1-back and croquet it to a spot about a yard south-west of the hoop. Make the hoop, perhaps gently roqueting yellow at the same time. Croquet it to whichever of the two positions you choose, obtaining a rush on red to such a position that it may be sent to 3-back while blue goes to the pioneer at 2-back. Somewhere near point x on the diagram is best, because you can miss it by quite a long way and still have a reasonable croquet stroke (but beware rover doesn't get in the way). Put red as near as you can to 3-back, but don't send it past the hoop.

It should be fairly straightforward to obtain a sideways rush to the vicinity of 3-back after running 2-back; if this is not forthcoming abandon the NSL and settle for putting the black somewhere south-west of the peg. You may still manage a reasonable leave – either the Old Standard Leave or the Diagonal Spread (which will be covered in the fourth and last of these articles). This let-out is the main reason for making 2-back off the partner ball: it is not impossible to arrange an NSL with the partner at 3-back, but you will probably find it less successful, and harder to compensate for slight loss of control.

If you have the rush to 3-back, take it and croquet black to a position about a foot east and two feet north of the hoop. Make the hoop using red, placing it just to the right of the hoop and a foot past. (Notice that you can't do this from just anywhere, so think about it before roqueting red!) Run the hoop just past red, roquet it gently and croquet it to its final position – hidden behind the hoop from the end of A-baulk, but rushable to hoop 1. It is not desirable to get it *too* close to the hoop. You should now be beside black; rush it to the boundary where it cannot be roqueted by the ball at the hoop, and leave blue so that black has a rush to yellow. Don't leave the balls so close together that there is a double target from B-baulk. (Wylie shows the rush pointing to about hoop 5, and Lamb has it pointing at hoop 4. Endless scope for discussion there!)

Now we return to the question of which position to choose for yellow. It is often lifted, which may seem to make its exact position a matter of little importance, but that is not so. After all, it may not be lifted! Position *a* in the diagram (about 6 to 8 feet from the boundary) is the easiest from which to pick up a break. You rush to the boundary, croquet blue to hoop 2, and obtain a rush to hoop 1; that is simpler than if yellow is in position *b*. Also it is annoying if you try for position *b* and fail as you may well do if the ground is dry and bare round the hoops: not only do you demonstrate your lack of control and lose your confidence in getting it right at 3-back, you may leave a very short shot from the end of B-baulk – albeit a dangerous one for your opponent to miss. I think the only reason to leave the ball in position *b* is to show off. Not that I decry such display!

The NSL is designed not to leave a short shot and to give an easy pick-up for the triple, especially if yellow is lifted and shoots unsuccessfully at black from B-baulk. Black gently roquets blue, takes off to yellow, and sends it to hoop 2 getting a rush on red to hoop 1. If you can't play that shot reproducibly, forget the NSL. The other snag is that your opponent doesn't need to play it. If he hits black reasonably solidly he can probably croquet it to hoop 2 stopping beside blue. The take-off to red is much easier than the shot out of corner IV.

Footnote. 'New' is a relative term. New College is over 600 years old and Newcastle 300 years older still. By such criteria the NSL is indeed 'new'. However, 'standard', according to Chambers, means 'of enduring value'; whether that is true for you or not, you can only find out for yourself in time.

I may be ten minutes late for the match; my husband's just dropped dead.

Late again! That's all you ever think of: croquet, croquet, croquet!

More domestic bliss

It's your turn to run a hoop

Ellicott and the triple peel

by DK Holland

"I have long contended," said my friend Ellicott, "that the triple peel, in all its forms, is the most gross manifestation of arrogance seen in croquet today."

Ellicott pursed his lips, glared at me, and bit savagely into another of the cream eclairs which invariably accompanied his otherwise nondescript luncheon.

"But you will allow," I responded tentatively, "that the triple peel, performed well, is a most difficult manoeuvre?"

Ellicott's brows shot together. The eclair was dropped to the plate. "Allow?" he thundered, "I will allow no such thing. And as for being difficult, so is standing on your head. To quote the great Dr Johnson: for a dog to walk on its hind legs is difficult, but one should not consider whether it is done well, but more to the point of whether it should be done at all. The triple peel, my dear DK, is simply a circus trick, and has no more place on a croquet lawn than heckling spectators in hob-nailed boots."

I should perhaps here explain a little about the general character of Ellicott. A fairly competent player of croquet, he was inclined to a relentless intimidation of his opponents via a long study of the Potter concept of One-upmanship. The Ellicott maxim was that if you were not One-up, you were, without question, One-down; and he pursued this philosophy come what may.

Ellicott's take-offs, for example, were notorious in that the ball from which he took croquet seldom shook, let alone moved; and his response to a questioning opponent was to swing his mallet menacingly and at the same time advance to within six inches of his questioner's nose. He would then tap his mallet a couple of times on the innocent turf and declare in a loud voice: "Moved!? You question whether it moved. Are you blind, sir? Or are you so desperate to win that you would resort to chicanery to put me off this splendid game I am playing?"

To be fair to Ellicott, there is no doubt that he really believed his ball had moved, and for all his bluster and gamesmanship, he had an untiring love for croquet and played it in a positive and spirited fashion. Not for Ellicott the game of Hide and Seek, and so-called 'percentage' croquet was anathema to him.

She's just taken off to 4-back.

I bit into my Huntley & Palmer biscuit and attempted to pursue the matter of the triple peel. I knew I had to be quick, and countered while Ellicott was sampling another sticky eclair: "Tell me, Ellicott, if the triple peel is such a bad thing or, as you say, an arrogant circus trick, why is it that so many of our up-and-coming players think it necessary to attain the skills required to perform it?"

"I will tell you why," Ellicott retorted. "It's because of the examples set by those who should know better. The few at the top set the standards, unfortunately, and they take delight in their childish high-wire act of proceeding to 4-back, wiring you, and then sucking their thumbs while you miss the lift. They then take their second ball around, perform their wretched triple peels, and believe in their naivety that that is how croquet should be played."

Ellicott drew in his breath, stifled the question hovering on my lips with an impatient wave of his hand, and continued with shoulders hunched forward confidentially: "And in any case, if they must show off, why not continue to rover with their first ball? Four balls placed accurately, one in each corner, is an admirable leave. But they either lack courage are are too besotted with their precious triple peel."

"You will agree that a triple peel can finish a game in a remarkably disciplined fashion," I ventured cautiously.

Ellicott's eyes bulged at this, and his reply was typically intense: "I can see, DK, that you are yet another unwitting accomplice to the lunacy that is rapidly sounding the death-knell of any universal embracing of our game. And as for the triple peel finishing the game with discipline, a thump on the offending player's head with a heavy mallet would do just as well — and create a lot more spectator interest into the bargain."

"Would you ban the triple peel?"

"The triple peel," Ellicott responded flatly, "must not be allowed to continue without the introduction of imaginative curbs on the player who attempts one. And there must also be revisions of the rules to allow compensating strategies to the other player."

Ellicott had finished his luncheon and now stared reflectively at his empty plate. "Croquet is, after all," he continued quietly, "a contest between two people. In singles anyway. And you will concede that a contest requires interaction?"

I nodded vigorously while stuffing myself with the last of the Huntley & Palmers. I knew that croquet was a game between two people. I had lost enough of them to know I wasn't playing by myself.

"But where is the interaction," Ellicott continued, poking a spoon aggressively into a cup of Gold Blend. "The circus clown wins the toss, elects to go in, stops at 4-back, sneers when you miss the lift, and goes out on a triple peel. Boring high-wire stuff. Utterly boring."

"I used to like seeing the odd circus or two," I responded excitedly. "And I tell you what, Ellicott, I never thought the high-wire acts were boring. Some of those buxom wenches in skimpy costumes don't half make a chap ..."

Ellicott's glare and admonishing wave of his hand cut me off in mid-sentence. "Take the American game," he continued soberly. "Lots of interaction there. They have their priorities right. They play to the spectators. They see croquet as a contest, not a one-sided exhibition by a computerised ghost in white."

Ellicott had now risen to his feet and was busily swinging his mallet in preparation for the next round of what he saw to be the Game of Life.

I had never yet got the better of Ellicott in any dialectic. I now thought I saw a chance.

"Ellicott!" I yelled after him as he was half way through the door. "Have you ever done a triple peel?"

Ellicott was stopped in his tracks. But I was mistaken if I though that the calorie-filled eclairs had in any way diminished the quality of his repartee.

"No, I have not," he responded affably. "I have always been too busy playing Croquet."

You will, Oscar, you will

I gain my pleasure in the game of croquet, not only from the play but increasingly from the conversation. I remember sitting watching a short-croquet competition at the Gateshead Garden Festival, in the company of Allan Ramsay from Edinburgh. The local organisers had done their best, but the 'lawns' had suffered somewhat from having been used also for children's football tournaments, and the occasional parachutist had alighted on them, trailing black ash from his boots. There was noise from everywhere, fortunately drowning the muttered imprecations of the players as yet another attempted rush turned into a roquet missed on the high side. "This reminds me of Cheltenham," said Allan. I raised the metaphorical eyebrow. "Oh, not the croquet club," he clarified. "More the Gold Cup course."

Another witty Scot is Malcolm O'Connell. We were playing at the Bush club one day when a passer-by released her long-haired dachshund from its leash. Those of my readers who have seen Dougal in "The Magic Roundabout" will need no further explanation of how it expressed its pleasure. The rest of you must try to imagine its joyous shakings, its transported dashings hither and yon.

"Oh, look," said Malcolm, "a hoop-cleaner."

Is this where they're holding the short croquet tournament?

Six and half a dozen

Those who have represented Great Britain and Ireland in the MacRobertson Shield or the Solomon Trophy are a select group, though they might not sound it from these clues. Can you identify these twelve? (Solution on page 89.)

It sounds as if he's wet – but you shouldn't cross him.
He has a victory about the end of September.
Listen; he might write the tournament report.
Leader of party – he's now a twitchy player.
Might he grunt in addressing the Queen?
He starts to win after long relaxed rest.

He'll have rye? Not he!
He has a kind of leave named after him.
This man *is* an island (in East Romania).
He's first in America, then steals back before everyone.
Quiet! Starting to roquet middle of tice's difficult for him.
He sounds as if he would like someone to give him a ring.

The evolution of man

The fascination of croquet

You're the croquet player, aren't you? Give him my turn; I'd rather wait for the politics, EC and weather man.

Advanced gadgetry

Constructing a WATCH

What I shall describe here is not too difficult, because few of the dimensions are critical, but you do need a vertical drill capable of drilling a hole $^{11}/_{16}$" in diameter to a depth of at least two inches. A friend with a milling machine would make everything rather easier.

The objective is to make a Wooden Appliance To Clamp Hoops. Various implements with such an aim exist, but the others I know of are either very expensive or, if you are going to make one yourself, need skills like welding, which few of us have. We shall therefore make a relatively simple but effective wooden one. The plan on the opposite page assumes that you have two pieces of hardwood 9" long by 1" by 2"; old teak flooring $4^{3}/_{4}$" wide is splendid if you cut it along its length, and that is what has been used to make the WATCH on page 93. Clamp the two pieces together so that you have a block 9" long by 2" square, and drill a hole $^{3}/_{8}$" in diameter through both pieces and centred $^{1}/_{2}$" from one end. Take out the wood between this hole and the end of the blocks, either by repeated drilling with one of these clever bits which drill square holes, by milling, or by sawing. Do the same at the other end.

Turn the block through 90° and drill a hole 3mm in diameter through one of the blocks so that it intersects the first hole drilled (yes, I know there are 6 ways of turning the block through 90° – see the plans). The exact place for this hole is $^{1}/_{2}$" from both the end and the edge of the block). This will take as a tight fit a $^{1}/_{8}$" diameter pin about an inch and a half long which will act as a pivot for a threaded bolt. Repeat at the other end.

Now separate the blocks, and, into what was the hidden face of the one with the small holes, drill two holes an inch and a half apart $^{1}/_{4}$" above the centre line and $^{3}/_{8}$" deep to take $^{3}/_{4}$" of dowel plug; this is usually 10mm diameter. Drill somewhat larger holes in the corresponding places in the other block. This refinement just makes sure that you define the 'top' of the clamp and always put the two parts together in the correct orientation.

Take a $2^{1}/_{4}$" long piece of $^{3}/_{8}$" diameter threaded bolt ('rodding') and drill a hole in it 4mm in diameter $^{3}/_{16}$" from one end; this is easier to do if you file the thread flat first. The rodding should be able to swivel freely on a $^{1}/_{8}$" diameter pin. Gently hammer such a pin through one of the small holes in the block and the hole in the bolt, with the bolt in place in one of the slots you have made. Put a butterfly (wing) nut on the other end of the bolt. One with a built-in washer is most convenient; if you cannot find one a loose washer is essential. Hammer the thread at the top of the bolts to stop the wing nuts from escaping. Repeat at the other end and hold the two blocks firmly together using these clamps.

Now comes the crucial part. Hoop uprights are $^{5}/_{8}$" in diameter, plus paint; this normally comes to $^{11}/_{16}$" or 17mm. If the width of the hoop is to be $3^{3}/_{4}$" (approximately 95mm) the distance between the centres of the holes which will clamp the uprights the correct distance apart must be $4^{7}/_{16}$" ($4^{13}/_{32}$" if you want to err on the narrow side) or 112mm. These holes, taking an equal amount of wood from each block, must be drilled very precisely.

Smooth off all the hard edges and apply a light coating of polystyrene varnish to protect against the damp grass you will encounter. Use pyrography to engrave your club logo on both halves to protect against the people from other clubs who will be envious of your WATCH.

Using the WATCH to set hoops is easy. Loosen the butterfly nuts, place the block with the nuts attached under a (horizontal) hoop, staying just clear of where the carrots join the uprights. Use the dowels to locate the other block roughly, swing up the clamps and tighten. Knock the hoop into the ground. You should now have a correctly set hoop, and your carefully graded balls should just pass through it – this is easier if you remember to take the WATCH off first.

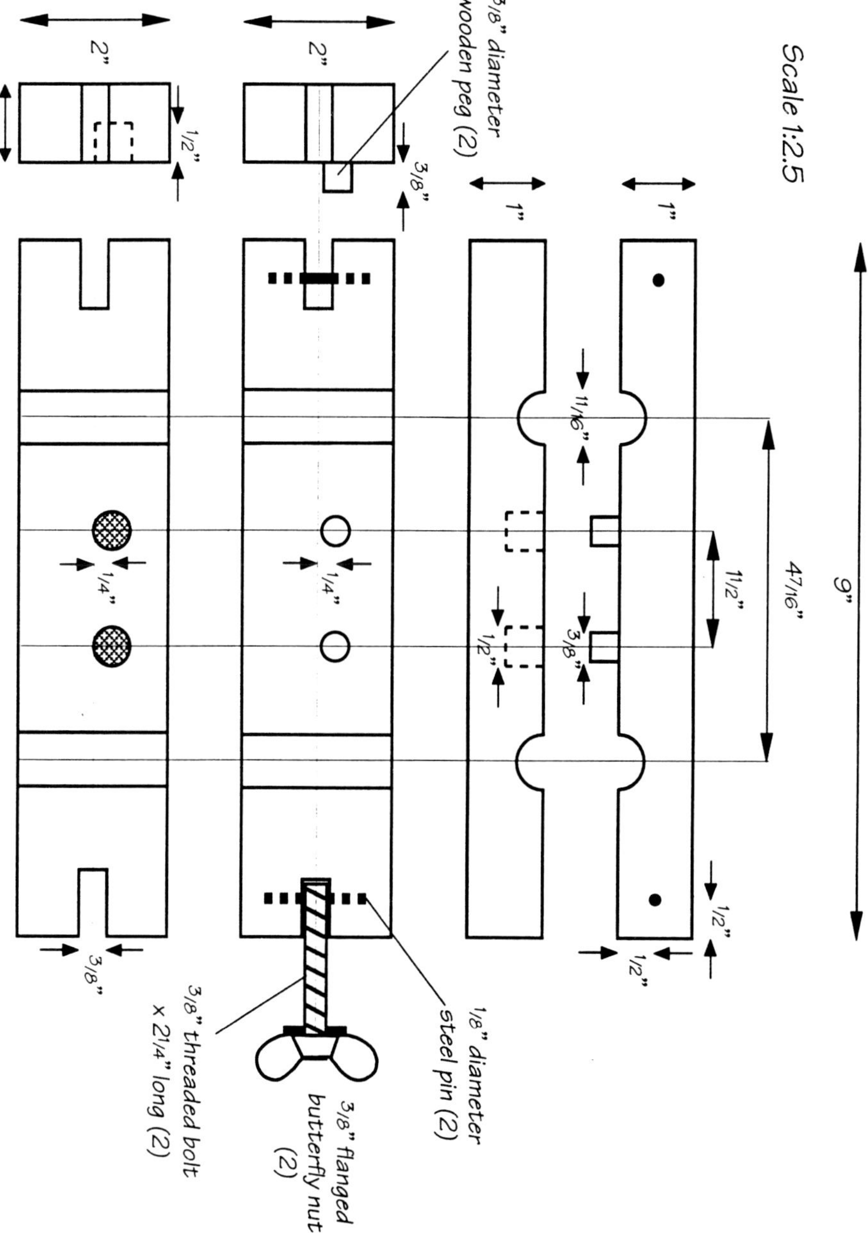

Coaching tips #4

Masters spread yourselves

Last, but (as they say) by no means least comes the diagonal spread. It's the safe one; it's the professional one. So what's it doing in here? Well, I suppose it is for when the wind is blowing the rain into your face and you just want to win the game and go and have a nice warm drink, whether it is tea or the Scottish equivalent. The lighter side of serious croquet quite often happens after the peg-out. So how does it go?

Let us suppose once again that you are playing blue and that you have reached 1-back, which you are making off your partner black. Red is between 1-back and the peg, and yellow is your pioneer for 2-back. After making your hoop croquet your partner ball just past the peg and rush the pivot, red, to wherever it is convenient to place it as a good pioneer at 3-back while going to the pioneer at 2-back. The rush you want out of 2-back is easier than the one you need for the NSL because it is back to the peg: one way of obtaining it is to put yellow quite deep and run the hoop to the boundary. You don't have to blast it through to get there, just a good firm stroke will do.

You take the rush to the peg and leave yellow maybe a yard south-east of it. You then either roquet your partner and take off to the ball at 3-back, or preferably rush partner past 3-back and croquet it back towards the peg. Its actual position is not absolutely crucial, but you should not get it too close to the peg or the other ball or leave it in the way of the croquet shot which comes after making 3-back.

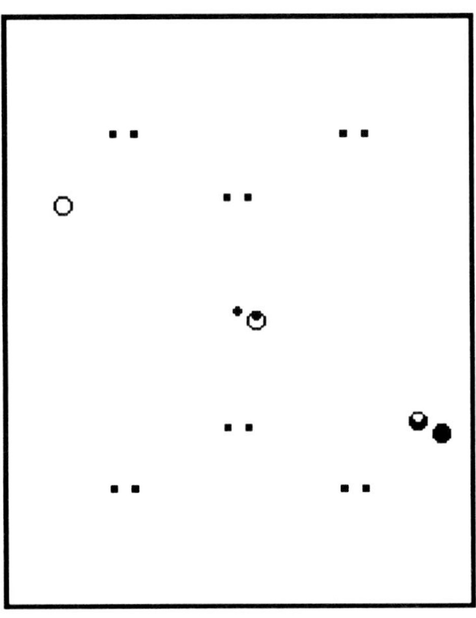

That shot involves placing the red in the position towards the west boundary as shown in the diagram and leaving the black close enough to red to roquet it into its final position. Of course it can be adjusted as you take croquet from it, but sad experience tells me that that is leaving it too late; you really want to take off from it so that it moves an inch or so nearer the peg and you get a rush on black to the east boundary. All this is made much easier by getting a decent rush out of 3-back. You can now see where you might want to have left black as a getaway ball for the final rush. The most embarrassing thing is to ricochet off it into the ball you have so carefully placed by the peg.

Of course all the balls and the peg should be in a straight line. Don't leave blue too short a rush or your opponent will have a double target from somewhere on B-baulk.

Croquet as religion

I don't wish to appear to be preaching to you, Miss Jones, but ...

The croqueted ball didn't move, Father.

It won't be long now; he's playing his doubles match at 11.45.

Oh, no! Guess who's just snuffed it.

The half-jump through rover

A croquet crossword by Dis

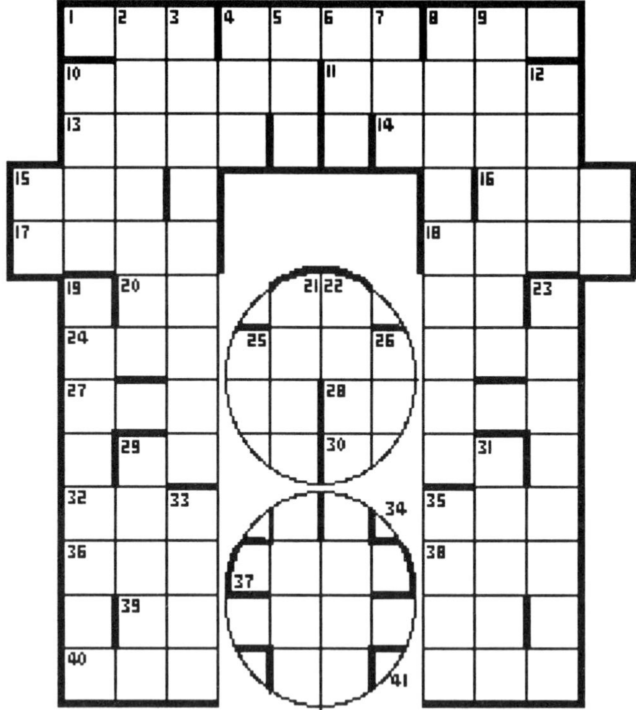

The ten 3-letter lights are of two kinds: the first four (in clue order) are of one kind, and the last six of another. (Solution on page 91.)

Across

1. Bush couple I made tipsy. Here? (6,5)
4. Mote – or moat possibly. (4)
8. He sits on the bench, but he tries suit with missing heir injudiciously. (10)
10. You gotta have this set of steps for audience. (5)
11. Quickly accomplished air attack contains Portugal. (5)
13. Comb until there are only traces of split ends. (4)
14. Manufactured using zero energy; that's kind of green. (4)
15. Listen to this! Drink for everyone, Sal! Rum cocktail with lots of ice. (7,5)
16. Rhetoric after small party in scientist's room. (10)

17. The earth leads to gravity and, implicitly, acceleration. (4)
18. You might get one, Arthur, with a Ford Prefect. (4)
20. Beneficial fluids, Artesian in origin. (8)
26. You could get these, alas, from phials – and snore. (10)
27. The place you and I must embrace the aforementioned woman. (5)
28. Winchester I fled from? (5)
29. Burn; small river in Scottish hillside. (4)
30. Cambridge periodical spurns grammar – that's close to way out. (4)
32. Large numbers of prizes. (4)
34. Deprive of essential tax. (4)
36. Just the greatest possible. (3)
37. Let this make a form of treacle. (4)
38. Fifty left out of roll-call reorganised into a band. (6)
39. Nicer glade has no shade surprisingly; trees have been cut down here. (8)
40. It's far from spring in June; April's nearer. (4)
41. Unknown number after employee. 32? (4)

Down

2. I put on a play 'The Political Optimist'. (7)
3. Heartless Don betrays anguished innocent one? (9)
4. Old fools ask EC for special treatment. (5)
5. Sorry mix-up about Henry starts and ends in pity. (8)
6. Object of respect. (7)
7. He came from Kent reading a higher degree in a year. (7)
8. What comes when the roller breaks? Two things the slow bowler needs. (9)
9. "Muriel, Ellen, Ann, every second counts." (Tyrone's such a wind-bag.) (7)
10. Where Zeno taught some ethics to Athenians. (4)
12. Diamonds bring forth the president of a trade-guild. (4)
19. Just blooming blew away inside old dwelling up north. (8)
21. Bad liar gets into nice mess? Quite the reverse. It's not causing trouble. (8)
22. Flowering twig, bitter vetch – and roses? (8)
23. Art of duper? Yes. (8)
25. Tangles with centre threequarters of football team. (4)
26. After viral infections this medication produces reddening. (4)
29. The Head is a plonker! (5)
31. Gail gets into a flap over new dress. (5)
33. Web, tissue, tale of deceit. (4)
35. This will warm things before getting up. (4)

The 14-point game

It seems to me that most players, including those A-class players who make mistakes, are happy with the 26-point game. It allows them to formulate strategies about the whole game, employ different tactics or styles of play during the game, and attempt varying kinds of breaks and leaves from the simple to those on or beyond the bounds of their capabilities. If the really good players are usually finished no later than the eighth turn and the game has turned boring for them, I sympathise while envying them their skill, but I cannot help but think that the shorter game (once round with each ball and hoops 3 and 4 as the lift hoops) will deprive them also of variety. Where will be the TPOs, the sextuples, the lengthy two- and three-ball endings which gather spectators around the lawn? I think the game is fun but ultimately lacking in satisfaction.

The debate about the 14-point game, the adoption of which the Croquet Players' Association has as its prime objective, needed encapsulating — at least my view that it was unsuitable for serious events did. It seemed appropriate to do this in 14 lines.

To one who would be his mistress

Thou pretty creature, lacking all deceit:
Although our friendship be but brief, 'tis true,
So dear delights do come of pastimes new,
And all our trysts (be they so short) are sweet.

The hours we spend together in the sun —
Of greater pleasures there can be but few.
But my affection do not misconstrue:
Alas, I cannot love thee, little one!

Thy older sister hath less verve, more guile;
How varied is her temper, cruel her art!
She makes me weep where thou dost make me smile,
And I adore her while she breaks my heart.

Around me still I pray her spell she'll weave.
'Tis her I love, and her I'll never leave.

Indoor croquet

I'll be glad when we've paid off these death duties.

Just like Smallwood. Plays in every event, and then vanishes when there's work to be done.

Bearing in mind we have to make 5 hoops in 10 minutes, I think the home team are playing for time.

How good a referee are you now?

(answers on page 87)

1. Jim sticks in 4-back, puts his clip on the hoop, and saunters back to his seat at the far end of the lawn. Before he has left the lawn his opponent, Bella, comes on from the north boundary and says "your ball's through 4-back, Jim"; what should the referee rule when he is called on to the court, assuming he confirms Bella's judgement?

2. Bert asks Darren to have a referee to watch the latter play a hampered hammer shot. The referee adjudges the contact to have been fair, but fails to notice the striker's ball brushing against Darren's foot after it has made the roquet. Does this matter? Can Bert do anything about it? Can Darren?

3. Roger wins the toss and puts Rupert in. Rupert lays a Duffer tice with red, but Roger ignores it and puts yellow on the east boundary. Rupert hits the tice with blue and sets up a break which he takes round to 2-back. Roger picks up black, notices the blue clip on the side of hoop 1, and puts two and two together. What should they do?

4. In an advanced game Bab is entitled to a lift. She lifts blue, which is in corner 4, then replaces it and plays black as it lies. Is this permissible? If not, has her opponent any redress?

5. With another referee you are sitting near the outplayer watching Jean play a break. A blatant double tap is heard by all. What action is open to the opponent? and to the referees?

6. Dennis accidently peels his partner ball (red) through hoop 1, but fails to notice and does not remove the clip. Senga sees it happen, but thinks she is not allowed to interrupt Dennis to draw it to his attention because no fault has been committed. When, some time later, Dennis runs hoop 1 with red, Senga apologetically tells him he is not entitled to a continuation shot because red is actually on hoop 2. Dennis is a bit peeved. What should the outcome be?

7. Just before Jill steps on to the lawn without having given the position much thought, a spectator says to her "that should be a nice one for a referee!". She deduces that she might have a wiring lift, and calls a referee to ask whether she is still entitled to ask for one. What do you tell her?

8. Elvis, playing with a personal stereo, is about to play his final stroke of a turn by joining up with his partner ball which has been moved by one of the double-bankers. His opponent attempts to prevent him playing, but Elvis cannot hear; he plays the stroke and strikes his partner ball. His opponent now succeeds by sign language in communicating with him, and together they ask a referee for advice. What should that advice be?

9. Pat takes croquet with yellow from black, and plays a legal but poor shot so that yellow is now prevented by black from roqueting blue. The three balls are all very close together. Her opponent requests that a referee be called to watch what he suspects will be a scatter shot. Pat asks the referee what she is likely to do that might be wrong. In what terms do you answer?

10. Yvonne and Belinda are playing advanced singles, though neither is experienced in that form of the game. Belinda has pegged out Yvonne's red, and Yvonne asks her if that means that Belinda will not be entitled to lifts for the rest of the game. Belinda says that is true, and Yvonne subsequently cleverly crosswires her opponent at 2-back and gets yellow in position for 1-back, wired from black and blue. Belinda asks Yvonne if she will agree to a lift; Yvonne says "you aren't entitled to one since you pegged me out"; Belinda explains she only meant lifts under law 36(a); Yvonne says she was playing while misled, and they call a referee. What should the referee do?

Cannon to right of them
Cannon to left of them

The four cannons I shall describe in this article all occurred in the Home Internationals in either 1992 or 1993. They are not therefore mere curiosities which only turn up in coaching courses: they can and do exert great influence on the results of matches at all levels. More than that, they are fun. They give players the opportunity to do something spectacular, and they exercise the brain just because they offer so many possibilities.

It is the cannon's opening roar

Quite often, if I am playing second, I will shoot at my opponent's ball on the east boundary. The third of these cannons deals with a case where I missed, but if I hit I will probably croquet my opponent up the east boundary about level with hoop 3, and then hit my own ball into corner I. My opponent has the choice of playing that ball, and probably not managing to move the short tice on the east boundary unless he successfully approaches and runs hoop 1, or shooting at the tice and risking giving me the innings if he misses. On the occasion in question, my opponent chose the second option and hit. He then took off to the ball in corner I, ending up short in the position shown in Fig 1; it was, after all, the first game of the day and he had had little chance to judge the speed of the lawn.

He should probably have retired to corner IV at this point, but he shot at my ball ... and missed. It was the fourth turn and I had a corner cannon. This is the most common cannon of all, and is very easy. You aim the croqueted ball about a yard to the west of hoop 2 (it will pull to the east), place the other ball to its right so as to make a right angle, and then strike in the direction of hoop 6 with sufficient strength to send the croqueted ball as a good pioneer to hoop 2. The other ball, which is roqueted in the stroke, should end up close to hoop 1. The exact place you should aim will depend on what stroke you use (Solomon suggests a slight roll, Lamb a drive; I prefer more of a stop shot). It will also depend on your mallet and the kind of balls you are using, but not a tremendous amount. It's worth the practice: I went to 4-back with a good leave, and felt a lot more relaxed.

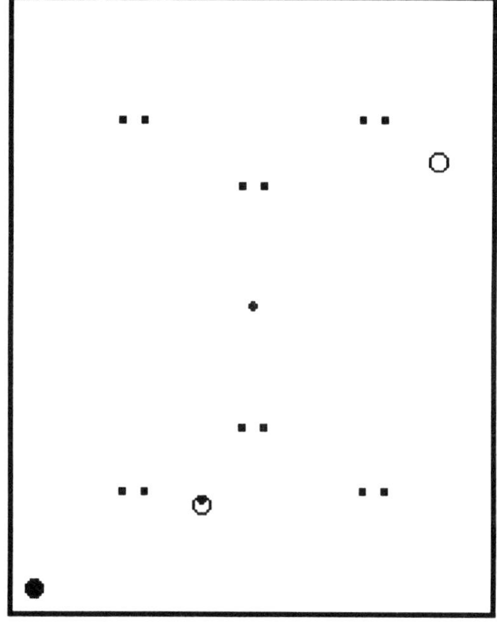

Fig 1

While they were content to peck cautiously at the ball, he never spared himself in his efforts to do it a violent injury.

The cannon I have just described is sometimes known as the half-crown cannon, because the space between the striker's ball and the roqueted ball is just the size of an old half-crown coin. But since I wish to attract younger readers who have never seen one, and since I hope also for foreign sales, I have defined the positions of the balls in terms of the angle they make. (Those of you with the necessary trigonometry, and armed also with the knowledge that the diameter of a half-crown was 1.25 inches, might like to prove that the half-crown cannon in fact gives an angle of 84°30'.)

At any rate, the space between the striker's ball and the roqueted ball in the next cannon is as small as you can make it: it is often called a wafer cannon. The one I want to describe came about from the position shown in Fig 2. My two balls were in contact in corner III; neither was actually on the corner spot, and they presented a target of a ball and a half to my opponent's ball 16 yards away beside hoop 6. This ball was wired from its partner which was beside hoop 4, and my opponent decided to shoot at me. This was on the aggressive side, as he probably wouldn't have got a cannon if he had hit, and it is doubtful if I could have done much if he had gone into corner II, but it was towards the end of a long, very hot day and he had already won the first game in the best-of-three, though I was on 1 and 4-back in the second. He missed.

If you line the balls up so that the croqueted ball is aiming about 3 yards south of hoop 2 and there is as small a gap as possible between the striker's ball and the remaining ball, then the line from the striker's ball through that ball points about a yard to the left of hoop 4. The possibility therefore exists to rush a ball to the ball by 4 while putting in a reasonable pioneer at hoop 2. Because of pull you will be doing well to get it within 5 yards of the hoop, but you would have to be pretty greedy to want more than that. The only two problems are where to aim and how hard to hit. For me, the second of these is pretty easy: I have to hit the ball just about as hard as I can unless the court is very fast, and on a slow lawn I can't hit it hard enough at all. Try going down the mallet a little to keep the shaft firm, aim between hoops 4 and 5 (nearer 4) and don't spare yourself. If you do it right you should be able to put the roqueted ball back into court and get a rush on the opponent to hoop 1. Which ball should you put at hoop 2: your own or your opponent's? I chose to use my partner ball as the pivot, thinking it would be easier to get it to 4-back for the peel. I stuck in a very tight hoop 2 off my opponent's ball, and lost. A sad little story.

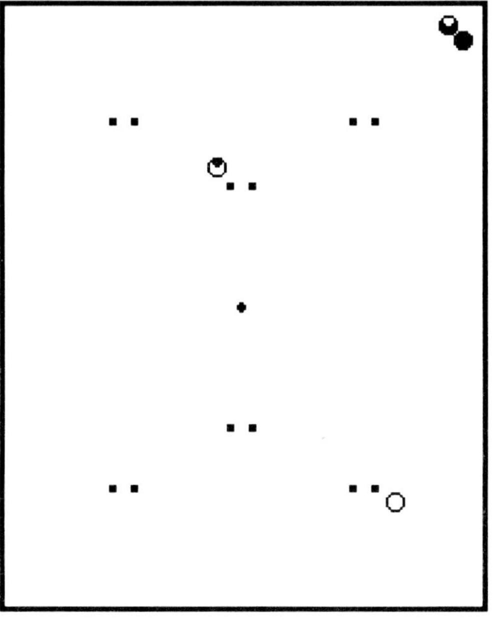

Fig 2

Promotion cometh neither from the east, nor from the west: nor yet from the south.

Even the source of this quotation can't get it right all the time: this cannon involves promoting a ball to hoop 1 from the east boundary. Again you have to hit quite hard, so perhaps Shakespeare is closer with "none will sweat but for promotion".

This happened in the match before the one in which the previously described cannon took place, but sadly I didn't get to play it this time. I had started by missing my opponent's ball, which was on the east boundary about 3 yards out of corner 4. Now, if you miss such a ball on the right by less than about 7 inches the balls will be in contact, and it can be important whether they are or not, so you should really have someone watch if you play such a shot. I did, it missed, they were. My opponent followed suit: the three balls were in contact. I missed the double target. These things happen: it's about the equivalent of a 7-yard shot at a single ball, and if I always hit those I would probably be out playing croquet instead of writing this!

So he had a 4-ball cannon, which he played to perfection and went round to 4-back. How exactly did he do it? Fig 3 illustrates how he set up the balls. It is another wafer cannon, but the fourth ball is promoted to hoop 1 without having been roqueted. The ball which is roqueted ends up between hoop 5 and the south boundary, from where it is possible to put it by the peg while going to the pioneer at 1. Be careful to aim the pioneer for hoop 2 two or three yards to the right of it: it will pull, and you don't want it to hit the peg.

The aiming point for your swing is hoop 4 or hoop 5: they are almost in line from where you play the shot. The promoted ball will be pulled south by the roqueted ball, so aim it a yard north of hoop 1. One of the good things about this cannon is that even if you leave the pioneer for hoop 1 well short you should still be able to get a rush on it and look as if that's what you meant to do all the time.

Bill Lamb (Croquet — The Skills of the Game, pp 58&59) gives another way to set up this cannon.

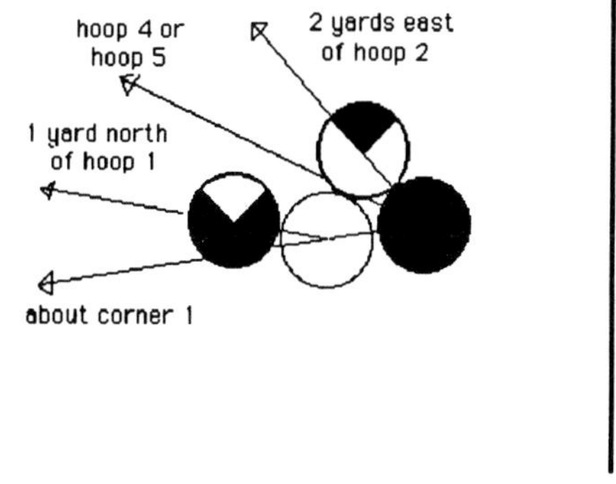

Fig 3

This thing was not done in a corner

The fourth, and last example of a cannon is not from one of my own games. The shot in question was played by Colin Irwin, and the play that led up to it was also of the highest quality. The balls were as shown in Fig 4 and it was David Openshaw (red and yellow) to play: he had few options and not surprisingly played red into corner II; yellow was on the north boundary a foot outside corner III. Colin took the 'rush' with blue to hoop 1 — it was actually about a 4-yard roquet — and got the rush out of the hoop to the red. He failed by about a foot to rush into the corner, but got behind the ball and made hoop 2 from it. He then rushed it back into the corner, stopped it out a little and got a rush on his partner ball into corner III. It looked as if he would manage to make that hoop too, but then things would get rather difficult; a break seemed some way away. Colin, however, played an open cannon; that is, in the stroke in which he put black to hoop 4 as a pioneer he roqueted yellow to within a yard of hoop 3, gaining enough control of the hoop to get the rush back to red, and suddenly there was the four-ball break and the potential delayed triple peel. The key shot was the open cannon, but it is not in fact as difficult as you might think. Try putting the blue in contact with the black as if it was an ordinary corner cannon like the first one I described, ie aiming it a yard west of hoop 4. Your line of swing is at the peg or hoop 1, and you play a stop shot. I hope you will be surprised at how successful you are. Of course, all the angles depend critically on the distance between the black and yellow, but if you practise this and the other three cannons intelligently you should be in a good position to generalise to whatever cannons you get in your next match. Have fun!

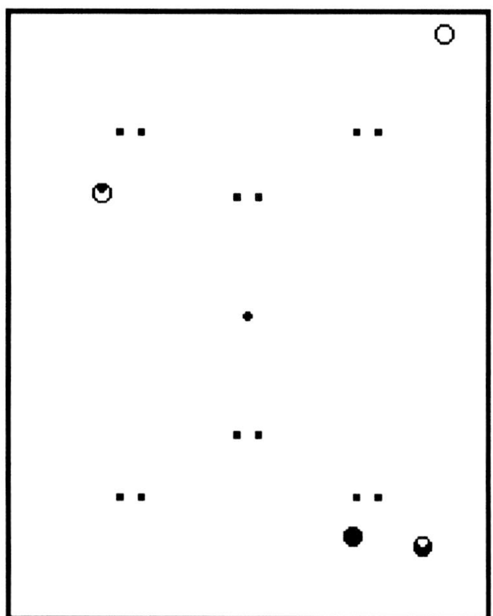

Fig 4

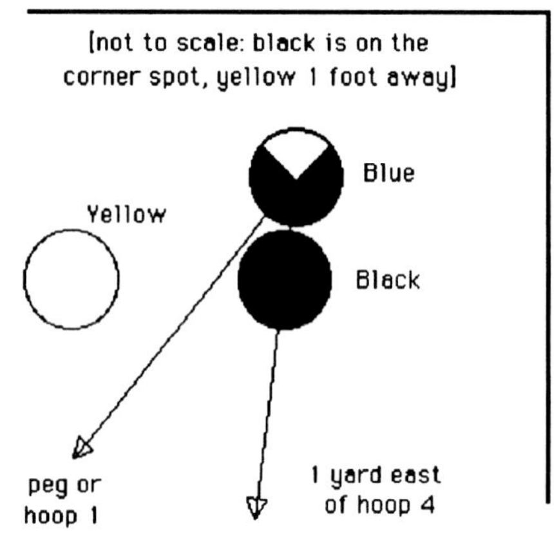

Fig 5

[If you have been wondering about the title and the subheadings, they are (i) Tennyson "The Charge of the Light Brigade", (ii) Byron "Childe Harold's Pilgrimage", (iii) PG Wodehouse "Chester Forgets Himself", (iv) The Prayer Book of 1662, (v) Acts of the Apostles. The Shakespearean reference on page 73 is to Orlando in "As You Like It".]

Croquet
and
Health
WARD 10
CORNER CANNONS
WARD 9
JUMP SHOTS
WARD 11
SPLIT SHOTS
DUST
BIN

A sextuple peel

The 'delayed' sextuple peel is the *ne plus ultra* of croquet breaks, and it is not given to many to perform it. The one I shall describe was done as a demonstration by world champion Robert Fulford after he had won the Australian Open title in Adelaide in 1994. He started from the usual position shown in the figure, which is reached from that in the article on leaves on page 7 after red has missed the 33-yard shot). Black's clip is on hoop 1 and blue's on 1-back.

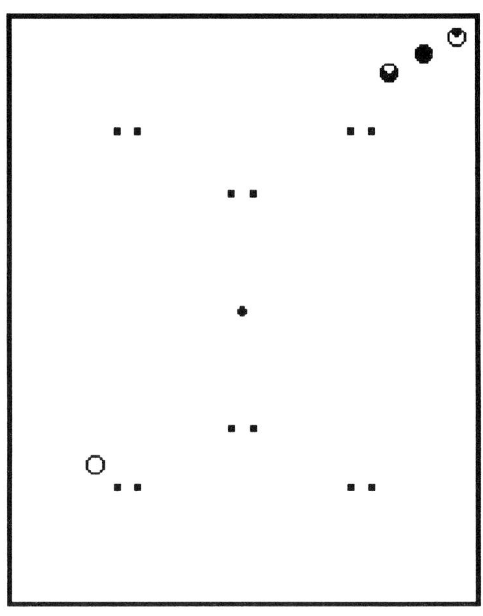

Robert roqueted red, stopped it out a couple of yards beyond hoop 3 and rushed blue into a possible peeling position at 1-back. He made no attempt to peel it, however, or even to put it into the jaws of the hoop; merely a take-off to yellow sitting by hoop 1, which was run with control to give a rush to beside red. Yellow was put into pioneer position at 3 and red rushed across behind blue and croqueted about 3 yards south of the hoop. This position allowed hoop 2 to be made and blue to be peeled firmly down to (indeed a yard or so past) 2-back, with black in a position to rush red towards the boundary north of hoop 3. One of the immaculate parts of Robert's game is that he hardly ever rushes off the lawn in such situations: he rushes instead to preferable positions a yard or two in from the yard-line.

So black went from such a position as a perfect pioneer to 4, and 3 was made with a rush on yellow towards corner 1. From between that corner and hoop 1 it was the placed as a pioneer for hoop 5; the position chosen was about 2 yards east by south east of hoop 1. Blue was roqueted in front of 2-back, but once again no attempt was made to peel it. The sheer lack of hurry to get the peels done was impressive! Those of us who can occasionally complete the six peels if we start with a ball in the jaws of 1-back want the 2-back peel done before hoop 2 is run, but no such panic here. Robert had previously told the onlookers to expect the 2-back peel before hoop 5, and he did not try to get ahead of this plan, though no doubt by putting the pioneer at hoop 4 deeper he could have done so. In any case he took off to this pioneer and once again got the perfect rush out of the hoop towards corner 1, whence red went to be the pioneer at hoop 6. But this was where things started to go slightly awry because the peel at 2-back stuck in the jaws of the hoop. Dawson mark 2 balls were being used, and they pull quite considerably and rather inconsistently; nor are they the easiest of balls with which to run controlled hoops.

However, the rush to 5 was achieved safely, so the break itself was still in perfect control, and out of the hoop yellow again went towards first corner, this time to be croqueted about three yards short of 1-back. Blue was rush-peeled through its hoop and split to 3-back as black went to make 6 off red. After 6 the rush was to corner 4 and the 2-back pioneer put in position some 3 yards north of the hoop: this was to prove important foresight, because the attempt at the 3-back peel with the big split roll going to the ball at 1-back was unsuccessful, the would-be peelee bouncing off the wire. Seven hoops made, but only two of the six peels. Surely it was all getting a bit too difficult.

There was also about a three- or four-yard roquet on yellow at 1-back, but that was no problem and another rush to corner 4 was obtained after running the hoop. The 3-back pioneer was then placed not at 3-back but just to the west of 4-back, and blue was successfully peeled about 7 yards up the lawn with a very thick take-off as black went to make 2-back. The rush from there was to near hoop 4 and red was sent west of 4-back as a pioneer. A perfect rush on blue was obtained and its execution was also superb: less than two feet from the hoop and right in front. The peel surprisingly only went into the jaws but the 3-back pioneer (at 4-back, remember) was then rushed to about two feet in front of 3-back and that hoop made. Some of the last few shots had been inch-perfect, but now it got a little tricky again: the attempt to get the forward rush out of 3-back left the black hampered by the hoop and only the power Robert generated in a very short distance behind the ball enabled the roquet to be made. Yellow went about a yard north-west of penultimate in the roll stroke and the blue was rushed through 4-back to the boundary from about three yards. Had it been left in the jaws as insurance? The roll would certainly have been harder if blue had previously gone through 4-back. Everything was back on course now for a straight double peel.

After 4-back was made red was put by the peg as black went to yellow; that was tucked up beside the hoop and position gained on blue, which had been croqueted from the north boundary to between yellow and penultimate. A stop-shot Irish peel sent the blue skimming past the peg and just beyond rover while black ran penult by a few inches. Yellow was roqueted out to the side and sent past rover, though only by about 4 or 5 yards, red was placed behind the hoop and blue rushed into ideal peeling position.

It then stuck in the hoop! A fall at the last fence? No, there was always the half-jump. Robert plays this shot well down the mallet, one of the few times he bends down; so down he went and sent the ball clean over the top of its partner to the boundary. What now? Sheer genius. He hit the rather long and somewhat cut roquet on yellow to about 4 feet in front of rover, bombarded blue a couple of yards through the hoop (to use the Australian expression), roqueted red, took off behind blue, rushed it up the lawn and pegged out both balls (in one stroke, naturally) from less than a yard.

It had been a superb exhibition of break play: of precision rushing, of placement of balls in case things went wrong, of delightfully accurate croquet strokes, especially round the hoops to get the required rushes out of them, and of delicate hoop-running. And let it not be said that there was no pressure to complete the break, because it was only a demonstration: if you lose to an opponent you can congratulate him on playing well; if you fail in a demonstration there is no-one to blame but yourself. Thank, you Robert: it was a joy to watch.

Rosemary and Basil go to time

My trouble is that I should really have been a *Guardian* sub-editor, but instead I ended up doing the job for the Scottish Croquet Association *Bulletin*. The opportunity for really awful puns is a bit limited, though some of my friends are kind enough to groan not infrequently.

It is, in fact, rather difficult to write a witty account of a weekend's croquet, and sadly few people try (though there are notable exceptions even apart from those mentioned here). They are mostly content to report the results and a few close endings and interesting shots, which has a certain limited entertainment value if you played the shots or know the protagonists, but otherwise has about the same impact as "Earth tremor in Japan – nobody hurt".

One of the exceptions is Andrew Gregory and his reports in *Croquet* have had some gems worthy of a more glittering setting. On one occasion Bill Lamb ('Coach of the Year' in 1991) was using a video camera to capture some playing styles for posterity. Andrew commented

> "If there's one thing worse than watching your opponent go round, it's watching a recording of your opponent go round"

(see page 61 of this publication).

He also hit the spot for me with

> "The weekend forecast was 'prolonged showers'. This turned out to mean bouts of rain heavy enough to warrant putting on waterproofs, and short enough to render this exercise pointless once complete."

His finest moment, however, was when hot-air balloons were observed during a weekend at Nottingham, and one got into difficulties. It looked at first as if the balloon might come down in the nearby lake, but in fact it landed safely on dry land not too far from the lawns. Andrew reports the occupants as saying that they were really aiming for a patch of grass just before the lake, and continues:

> "We don't think they meant the lawns, but it's an awful thought. It might give rise to the ultimate hampered shot."

Robert Prichard was a player of international quality who never forgot that, while the point of croquet is quite lost if you don't try to outwit and outplay your opponent, nevertheless what we are privileged to enjoy so much is a *game*. He also added atmosphere to his descriptions of play.

> "Entering the Hurlingham summer tournament can be like ordering drinks in a New York bar. The nine events with staggered starting dates give players a wide choice of personalised cocktails, depending on their thirst for play, taste for doubles (mixed or not) or singles, laced with bisques or neat."

Modesty does not prevent me from pointing out that I have twice written reports entirely in verse, but space prevents me from reproducing them here. I will end with a phrase which I stole from a real sports reporter to put in the *Bulletin*, and it is a mere coincidence that we were both writing about Glasgow:

> "It was the sort of day that Noah made famous" (or is it "... made Noah ...?).

Croquet widows

... then I took off to four-back, ran the hoop leaving me a perfect rush on red, then ...

Are you going to stay there all day sulking, just because I wouldn't let you go and play croquet again?

Brian! For the last time: I'm not interested in learning how to set up a four-ball break.

Because I don't want to play golf like other husbands.

The modern scientific game

I was recently lucky enough to be able to read a copy of *A Pocket Guide to Croquet, being a manual of the modern "scientific" game* by GH Powell of the Inner Temple. This book was published with the 1899 revision of the laws of croquet, and somewhat surprisingly Powell does not figure in Prichard's history of croquet. Here are some extracts from this most interesting publication, which show how essentially similar today's game is to the version created when the Croquet Association was formed a hundred years ago.

For example, the four-ball break is no new invention:

> The essence of the best play, in any game, is to utilize all the resources of that game. Which is precisely what the "four-ball break" does for croquet. So that, though the game may be played and won without much knowledge of this principle, a thorough understanding of it is absolutely necessary to Tournament play.

Incidentally, the book talks of tournament play taking place "from Budleigh Salterton to Edinburgh."

One point of difference was the mallet. The author pointed out at some length the illogicality of the law, feeling that either indiarubber should be banned or allowed for all strokes; but this is what it said:

> Mallets may be of any size, weight, or material. The two ends of the head must be parallel, and of equal size and similar shape. An indiarubber end may be used in taking croquet only. No point or roquet made by a stroke of an indiarubber end shall count.

I had not realised that in advocating that the opponent ought to have a choice after a fault of playing the balls as they lay or having them replaced, I was asking for the *reintroduction* of the following law:

> If a player make a foul stroke, he loses the remainder of his turn, and any point or roquet made by such stroke does not count. Balls moved by a foul stroke are to remain where they lie, or be replaced, at the option of the adversary.

There were, of course, some major differences in the laws from those we know now. Perhaps we need to reintroduce the turning peg (with no extra stroke for hitting it) to make the game harder for the top players:

> One of the pegs is known as the "turning", and the other as the "winning" peg.

The turning peg was half way between hoops 2 and 3, and the winning peg half way between hoops 1 and 4. Hoops 5 and 6 were closer together than they are now. However, the main difference in the laws was that the "sequence game" was still in operation:

> The balls, which are four in number, and coloured respectively blue, red, black, yellow play in that order, blue and black forming one "side" (whether there be two players or four) and red and yellow the other.

This makes it all the more surprising that basic tactics should be so similar to today's. How about this for good advice on defence?

> And of the whole extent of the boundary, the safest part is obviously *the corner*, which *the concurrence of two boundary lines* renders the most difficult spot to approach. Hence, throughout the whole game, there is but *one rule of policy* for a single ball detached from

> its partner, and in an absolutely unpromising situation, and that is *to play into a corner*. This is technically called *finessing*.

Or this on the leave?

> Thus, towards the conclusion of any "turn" in croquet, the player should always consider how far the hoops and pegs, the "furniture" of the court, can be utilized as a means of shelter or defence against the adversary.

Pegging out an opponent was even more of an advantage in the sequence game than it is now, but this still rings true.

> So crushing, in fact, is the advantage obtained by eliminating one of your opponents altogether, that a great risk is sometimes run to obtain it — failure, of course, meaning very possibly the inversion of the process.

Bisques were in use, and a tactic for using them in doubles (which took me a long time to realise — I wish I had read this book years ago!).

> When, for example, one of your opponent's balls has laid a fine four-ball break for the other, step in, and, according to your ability, appropriate it.

> Finally, in foursomes, the stronger hand should always be entrusted with the taking of the bisque.

They took care then about who was allowed to play in which tournaments.

> When the programme includes an open competition and a competition confined to Ladies, no competitor shall be eligible for both.

And etiquette was important. I am sure I have been addressed in the very words used in the next extract. Oh dear, I may even have used them myself!

> So, also, though you may individually be boiling over with sympathy for an antagonist who has the game all his own way, do not *express* your anxiety that it (*i.e.*, your own collapse and his success) "must all be rather poor fun for him," or words to *that* effect. Very possibly it is nothing of the kind, though his enjoyment may be impaired by the remark. It is bad form, even *to appear to lose interest in a game in which you are being worsted;* more especially if that game be croquet where "collapse" is about as common as seasickness in the Channel.

There are times, like in that last sentence, when we are reminded that the book was written while Victoria still reigned, and the following extract strengthens our contact with the 'Alice in Wonderland' style of croquet which had existed not so long before.

> A player who roquets a ball must take croquet, and in so doing must move or shake perceptibly both balls. If the two balls do not touch before, and in the act of, taking croquet, the adversary may claim that the stroke be made over again. In taking croquet, the striker is not allowed to place his foot on the ball.

However, this advert is the most distancing of all.

> **THE "ELITE" SET, for Eight Players,** comprises eight superior French Polished Boxwood Mallets, with octagonal handles, eight best quality Boxwood Balls, 3⁵/8 in., to match, seven ¹/2 in. Iron Hoops, improved pattern, Boxwood Hammer, Iron Drill, special Clips, Starting and Turning Posts, and copy of Slazenger's "Laws of Croquet." In strong Polished Pine cut-open Box, with brass lock and mountings.

The cost was three guineas.

Three trophies

It might seem a little surprising to mention trophies in a book dedicated to enjoying oneself, but even apart from the fact that it is nice to win, especially for ones country, the annual fixtures between the CA and the Scottish and Irish associations are among the most relaxed and enjoyable matches I have played in. They truly are the lighter side of serious croquet and a suitable finale to this book.

There is an effort made to match the playing strengths of the sides so that everyone finds the encounters interesting, and there is also the satisfaction of playing this most individual of sports in a team context for a change. It really is agreeable to play doubles with a partner who is normally one of your arch-rivals.

The CA and the SCA compete for the Glasgow Quaich, perhaps appropriately a large pewter drinking bowl; the CA and the CA of Ireland play for the McWeeney trophy, a handsome silver cigar case; I had the pleasure of designing and presenting the trophy for the match betwen the CAI and the SCA. It is a sterling silver set of a mallet, hoop, peg and two balls mounted on a lignum vitae mallet head on which appear the thistle of Scotland and the shamrock of Ireland.

Solutions to quizzes, crosswords and other puzzles

Answers to a Croquet Quiz

1. The MacRobertson Shield is named for Sir Macpherson Robertson, Australian confectionery manufacturer and philanthropist, who presented it in 1925.

2. England and the United States of America play for the Solomon Trophy, though the latter have yet to win it.

3. The trophy for the annual CA v SCA match is the Glasgow Quaich, presented by Glasgow City Council. The match was instituted in 1975; England won in 6 successive years from 1979 to 1984, but Scotland then fought back with 6 wins of their own. After the tied match in 1995 the CA lead by $10\frac{1}{2}$ to $8\frac{1}{2}$.

4. The world champions have been Joe Hogan (NZ, 1989), Robert Fulford (England, 1990, 1992 & 1994), John Walters (England, 1991) and Chris Clarke (England, 1995).

5. Croquet was played at the Paris Olympics in 1900; all the contestants were from France.

6. Martin Murray played in the Home Internationals every year from 1980 to 1995, with the exception of 1989. Scotland's only win to date was in the very first contest, when their captain was Stephen Wright. In that year only Scotland, England and Wales took part, and the deciding match was between Scotland and England at Nottingham. Murray beat Nigel Aspinall (that year's CA President's Cup winner), Andrew Hope beat reigning English Open Champion David Openshaw, and Wright beat the runner-up in that championship, Bernard Neal. The final match, between Keith Ross and Eric Solomon (the current holder of the President's Cup), was abandoned as a draw at one game all.

The report of the encounter written by John Solomon for the *Croquet Gazette* is interesting in many ways, not least for his criticism of Martin's use of the 'new standard leave' (and also, by implication the 'diagonal spread'), and his query "Does Martin stand too far back from the ball and therefore have to lunge to reach it?" [Yes, he does! See the photographic evidence.]

7. Nigel Aspinall won the English Open 8 times and Humphrey Hicks won it on one fewer occasion.

8. The photograph is of the Moffat Ram, which stands in the main street of the picturesque Dumfriesshire village where the Scottish Open was held in the 1870s; the trophy for the winner of the Scottish Open is the Moffat Mallet which bears the date 1871.

9. The Prichards (Robert, Colin and William) have been the backbone of the Welsh national side; Colin used the alias Eamon Holiday. William has been most successful, playing in four MacRobertson Shield sides.

10. Terence Read won the Championship of Ireland 9 times in succession from 1972 to 1980; Cyril Corbally had previously won it 8 times between 1901 and 1924.

11. Lt Cdr Sinclair won the All-England Handicap Tournament in 1967. The final was played at Hurlingham, and the winner was presented with his trophy by the Queen, as shown in the

photograph. This was the year in which (for some reason) the Croquet Association celebrated its centenary, and when raiders from north of the border also won in the following three years there were comments made! The *Croquet Gazette* records in 1970: "Once again then the trophy, albeit the All England Trophy, went to Scotland. Miss Lintern in presenting the prizes commented on Scottish croquet and handicaps in particular, and Mr MacLean in reply said that he would not like to say much about Scottish croquet, but sportingly conceded that the Scottish handicappers were very good for the Scots!" It should be noted that it may be the English who have brought their handicaps into line: in the 1970 finals John Solomon was playing off -5 and Bernard Neal, whom Bob MacLean beat in the final, off -4.

12. I took the photograph in Wellington after a friendly match with Paul Skinley, who had earlier in the season completed triple peels in 11 successive matches. Though Paul's triple failed against me he still won.

13. Allan Cleland from Victoria,who is a teacher, won his first Australian Championship in 1992 – though he had won at Sonoma in 1990. Tea flows even more freely in Australian croquet circles than it does in Britain; the photo is of Allan at one-all in his semi-final.

14. Graham Beale of New Zealand had a sextuple peel at Sonoma-Cutrer in 1987. His compatriot John Prince was first to complete one in competition (in 1970) and had two in a day in 1985. Yet another New Zealander, Bob Jackson, has performed 3 octuple peels.

15. Sonoma-Cutrer is in California, and is the site of the world's richest croquet tournament; Chattooga, where there is an annual contest between national Open Champions, is in North Carolina.

International section

English: a thick take-off.
jam at 1-back.

French: un pastiche idiot.
confiture à un dos.

How good a referee were you?

1. The roquet stands. Law 29d makes it incumbent on the outplayer to forestall play when the ball should have been played from a baulk line. Only in the unlikely event that Dan makes a habit of such strokes should regulation 5j be invoked.

2. It is irrelevant whether the ball hit the peg before or after the other one left the lawn. Law 31c defines the end of a stroke as the moment when all balls moved have come to rest or have left the court; the peg point may therefore be scored even if the other ball has left the court, though the turn, of course, ends under law 20c(1). However, the decision whether to remove the striker's ball from the lawn depends on (i) whether the striker's ball is a rover (law 15), and (ii) whether the game is being played under the laws of handicap play, in which case the striker's partner ball must also be a rover (law 39) — unless Steve had a brainstorm and was trying to peg out his opponent's only remaining ball! Nothing must be taken for granted, and the referee must make himself aware of all relevant facts.

3. Red must be replaced on the yard-line as the turn has ended under law 20c(1); see laws 12a(2) and 11.

4. Had one of the two matches involved bisques and the other not, there might have been more of a problem. It is probably satisfactory in this case to toss a coin to determine which match is being played (law 51).

5. Although one could say that this is a case of the wrong player playing the right ball, it must be treated as playing the wrong ball. Nothing irregular took place until Bill played the black — he was allowed to place it for partner (law 40b, by implication, or laws 36a(2) and 40(c)) — so black is replaced where he placed it (law 28b(1)).

6. Law 33 applies if all the balls had stopped or left the lawn, otherwise law 34.

7. The corner ball is replaced in the corner; Syd's ball in any legal position to take croquet from the corner ball, but not in the yard-line area (law 28b). The two bisques he took after playing the wrong ball are restored, but not the one he took before he played it (law 38h(2)). He can take another bisque to play with the correct ball (law 38a), in which case his ball is in hand (law 16c(1)) and may be placed anywhere in contact with the corner ball for the croquet stroke.

8. The opponent is wrong. Charlie has played when not entitled to do so, and the ball is replaced (law 27a applies, see law 38d(1)). A spectator referee may intervene under regulation 8b.

9. Yes, to both questions; law 38a only says a point may not be scored in a turn following a half bisque; law 14c allows the point to be made, since the ball has not become a ball in hand (unless in the subsequent stroke it is touching another ball, law 16c(1)).

10. Such a referee is a referee on appeal. He may not decide that a fault has been committed (regulation 7d) unless a spectator referee has observed the fault and passes on this information on request (regulation 7b).

A four-ball break

How good a referee were you this time?

1. Whether he has left the court or not, Jim has indicated that his turn has ended, and the ball is therefore deemed to be at rest (law 22b(4)); hence it is replaced under law 22a and the point is not scored. Since Bella may be about to shoot at a ball in a hoop, the referee should remain on court.

2. The stroke is a fault under law 32a(13) and law 31c. Darren can declare it as such (regulation 5b); likewise Bert may inform Darren that he thinks a fault has been committed (law 45b) and ask the referee to explain the law to Darren (regulation 5f). The referee cannot decide that a fault was committed unless Darren declares it, since he did not observe it, unless he consults a spectator referee who has seen the fault.

3. Rupert's error has not been condoned, so the correct ball would normally be placed on a Baulk line (law 28b(1)), but because of Roger's previous error, which has been condoned, that is impossible. Law 28c therefore applies and the game is restarted.

4. By lifting blue, Bab has opted to play the turn with it (law 8b(2)) and may not then change her mind (law 8c), so law 28b applies and her opponent has redress unless he has played the first stroke of his next turn.

5. The opponent may draw attention to anything he believes to be a fault (law 45b) and summon a referee on appeal who may act under regulation 7a; that referee may consult the other referees (regulation 7b). Notice that only a single referee may be consulted; in response to a general appeal only one should respond.

6. Senga should have notified Dennis of the misplaced clip (law 45b); Dennis may justifiably claim to have been playing while misled and should begin his turn again (law 35a(1)).

7. Under law 49a, Jill may not take advantage even of unsolicited information; you must tell her that she may not ask for a lift if she had not considered the possibility before the spectator's comment.

8. By continuing to play after his opponent had forestalled play (law 26a), Elvis is subject to law 27, and the stroke is invalid. The balls should be replaced and the stroke replayed.

9. You may tell Pat that the next stroke is a continuation shot, and that since the balls are close together, hitting black may lead to a double tap (law 31a(9)) which would be illegal, though it would not be a fault if she were roqueting it; you may also enumerate other possible faults, such as striking the ball with any part of the mallet other than the end-face, if you consider the stroke hampered (law 32a(5)); you may not give advice about how to avoid such faults (regulation 5f).

10. Yvonne was playing when misled (law 35b), and should be allowed to play the whole turn again. Would it be unreasonable to let her replay only part of the turn (eg after hitting in; or the final stroke, thus maintaining the crosswire at the expense of poorer hoop position, even if the crosswire had been accidental)?

I now claim the match due to you taking too long to play your shot.

Run rover

The diagrams on the right may help. If not, they are followed by full instructions in what I hope is a self-explanatory notation. I give no guarantee that the solution is optimal, and indeed would be pleased to hear of any substantial improvement. Since I estimate that to take a ball round to 4-back and then perform a triple peel takes in the region of 130 strokes, this puzzle, with about the same number of moves, may be taken to be of similar difficulty!

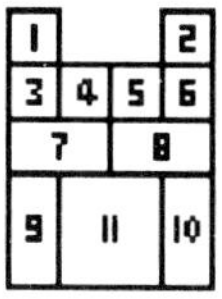

Diagram 1

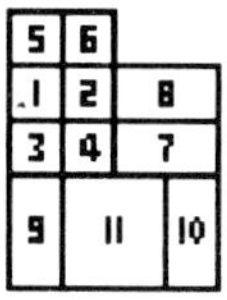

Diagram 2

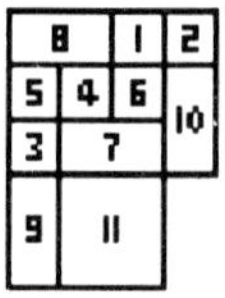

Diagram 3

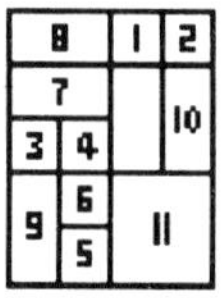

Diagram 4

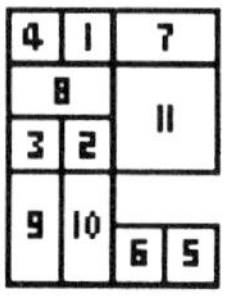

Diagram 5

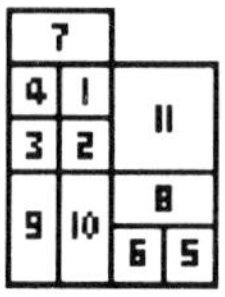

Diagram 6

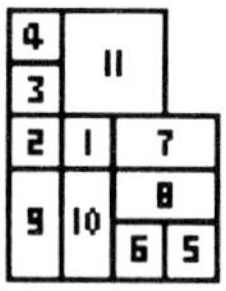

Diagram 7

2W2; (5,6,8)N; 7E2; (3,4,1,2)S; (5,6)W2; we are now at diagram 2 – ok so far?

8N; (1,2)E2; (5,6)S; 8W2; (1,2)N, 6E; 4N; 7W; 10N2; at last the ball can move – diagram 3.

(11,9)E; (3,5)S2; 7W; 6S; 4E; 7N; 5NE; 3N2; 9W; 5S2; 6SW; 4SW; and we are at diagram 4.

10W; 2S2; 1SE; 8E2; 7N; 4NW; 10W; 2NW; 11N; 5E2; 6SE; 10S2; 2SW; 1W2; 8S; 7E2; (4,1)N; 8W2; 11N; great! the ball has now moved two positions nearer the hoop – diagram 5.

6NE; (10,9)E; 3S2; 2SW; (8,4,1)S; 7W2; 11N; 8E2, 2NE; 3N2; (9,10)W; 6SW; (8,11)S; what? we're moving away again. Not to worry: croquet players should be used to going in an apparently wrong direction to set up the rest of the break. It won't be long now – we're at diagram 6.

7E2; (4,1,3,2,9,10)N; (6,5)W2; (8,11)S; (2,3)E2; (4,1)S; 7W2; (3,2)N; (1,4)E2; 7S; (3,2)W2; (4,1,11,8)N; (5,6)E2; (9,10,7,3,2)S; (4,1)W; 11N; 7E2; 2SW; 1S2; 11W; and from diagram 7 the ball runs rover!!

Bob Race crossword

1 M	A	2 C	R	3 O	B	4 E	R	5 T	S	6 O	N	■
A	■	L	■	V	■	T	■	I	■	N	■	7 S
8 L	E	A	V	E	S	■	■	9 C	H	E	A	T
L	■	S	■	R	■	10 O	■	E	■	B	■	A
11 E	A	S	Y	L	I	F	E	■	■	12 A	L	L
T	■	■	■	O	■	F	■	13 T	■	C	■	K
■	14 R	15 O	U	N	D	B	R	E	A	K	S	■
16 S	■	U	■	G	■	L	■	N	■	■	■	17 P
18 P	A	T	■	■	19 A	U	N	T	E	20 M	M	A
L	■	S	■	21 S	■	E	■	O	■	O	■	S
22 I	R	I	S	H	■	■	23 R	O	Q	U	E	T
T	■	D	■	O	■	24 U	■	N	■	S	■	E
■	25 S	E	X	T	U	P	L	E	P	E	E	L

Six and half a dozen

Fulford [sounds like full ford]
Irwin [I WIN about R]
Clarke [sounds like clerk]
Openshaw [anagram (twitchy) of P+HE'S NOW A]
Maugham [UGH in MA'AM]
Walters [W + anagram (relaxed) of A+L+REST]

Avery [HAVE+RYE -HE]
French (leave)
Mulliner [MULL IN E+R (vehicle registration)]
Aspinall [A+NIPS (reversed)+ALL]
Prichard [P+R+IC+HARD]
Saurin [reference Sauron in 'Lord of the Rings']

Answers to short croquet crosswords

1 S	I	2 R
P	■	E
3 A	I	D

1 *ac*. siren - en=quad(rat).
3 *ac*. hidden (in reverse) in **dia**gonal.
1 *dn*. satisfies **p**layers' **a**mbitions.
2 *dn*. scared - SCA.

1 T	E	2 A
P	■	I
3 O	A	R

1 *ac*. hidden in 'mos**t** **Ea**ster' & 'la**te** **A**utumn'.
3 *ac*. 'stroke' as in boat-race & anag. (duff) **or a**.
1 *dn*. t=time + p=Prince + **O**pens; *I* think it's high-risk.
2 *dn*. hairy - H=henry - Y=yellow.

1 L	E	2 T
U	■	I
3 D	I	E

1 *ac*. 2 meanings.
3 *ac*. 2 meanings.
1 *dn*. (as in m'lud); ludo - O=nothing.
2 *dn*. tice - **c**rucial.

1 A	I	2 L
C	■	A
3 T	I	P

1 *ac*. Gail - **g**enius.
3 *ac*. triple - rover peel failu**re**.
1 *dn*. contact - **c** - on **t.**
2 *dn*. pal backwards.

1 O	A	2 F
W	■	I
3 L	A	X

1 *ac*. loaf - **L**.
3 ac. 3-letter code for Los Angeles airport.
1 *dn*. howler - her.
2 *dn*. 3 meanings.

Dis crosswords

The clues to the first four 3-letter lights lead to PUBLIC HOUSE, SUBSTITUTE, POPULAR MUSIC and LABORATORY; the solver must enter the appropriate abbreviation.

The next six lead to
(ONE &) ALL,
COLLAR (& TIE),
CAKES (& ALE),
(TEA &) SYMPATHY,
(ORB &) SCEPTRE and
(MAN &) SUPERMAN.

The idea was taken from a crossword by Alastair Hunter of Glasgow Croquet Club. The clue for 20 across appeared in an Azed crossword in the 'Observer'.

	P	U	B	A	T	O	M	S	U	B	
	S	T	Y	L	E	R	A	P	I	D	
	T	O	S	E	A	B	N	I	L	E	
P	O	P	T	—	—	—	—	N	L	A	B
G	A	I	A	—	—	—	—	D	E	N	T
	N	A	N	T	I	S	E	R	A	P	
	E	N	D	O	R	P	H	I	N	S	
	W	H	E	R	E	R	I	F	L	E	
	B	B	R	E	N	A	N	T	A	U	
	L	O	T	S	I	Y	G	E	L	D	
	O	N	E	A	C	E	R	T	I	E	
	W	C	L	E	A	R	I	N	G	R	
	N	E	A	P	L	S	M	A	N	Y	

R	E	S	I	T	S	A	L	L	A	B
O	O	R	K	N	I	P	T	O	I	R
E	●	A	E	A	S	Y	●	T	O	O
T	R	N	S	E	O	G	E	S	I	W
I	O	I	U	T	N	O	T	I	O	N
H	G	D	F	A	E	L	A	P	S	E
W	I	P	E	G	■	O	U	T	R	E
H	O	O	D	O	O	L	E	T	A	●
E	N	D	I	N	G	L	L	I	R	T
Y	D	R	G	E	R	I	D	B	A	N
A	I	A	●	E	E	R	D	R	B	E
R	R	W	L	L	E	B	O	O	A	R
B	E	N	I	G	N	I	N	W	A	Y

The solution diagram shows the secondary colours and the peg-out. Notice that the initial letters of the flags are in the corners. That was meant to help! On the other hand, N appears in the middle of the south boundary and S in the middle of the north one. That wasn't!

Loose ends

There are occasional literary allusions throughout the book, and I wouldn't like my readers to lose too much sleep over them. Those in the article on cannons are explained at the end of that article; here is some help with the others.

In Jane Austen's *Persuasion* Sir Walter Elliot found "occupation for an idle hour" in looking himself up in the *Baronetage*. (page 2)

Tennyson had the eponymous hero claim "My strength is as the strength of ten, Because my heart is pure" in *Sir Galahad.* (page 4)

The improving story of the Amorites' defeat is in the tenth chapter of the book of Joshua. (page 4)

"This life is a journey we a' hae to gang, And care is the burden we carry alang" is an observation, not of Burns but of the Paisley poet Robert Tannahill in *A Wee Drappie O't.* (page 4)

Susan Warner gave life to *Jesus Bids Us Shine* which contains the line "You in your small corner, and I in mine." (page 22)

It *was* Burns who was responsible for "despising wind and rain and fire" and "the de'il had business on his hand" in *Tam o' Shanter.* (page 24)

"Most musical, most melancholy" is Milton: *Il Penseroso.* (page 28)

"Remember, o man, that thou art dust" is from the liturgy for Ash Wednesday. (page 28)

James Whistler suggested Oscar Wilde was not always original. (page 59)

"Masters, spread yourselves" is Bottom's exhortation to his friends in *A Midsummer Night's Dream.* (page 64)

I hope you enjoyed the book and enjoy the serious and lighter sides of your croquet.

The 'solution' to the plans

The CATAPULT in use when the edge of the court is marked by string. The ball is just off the court.

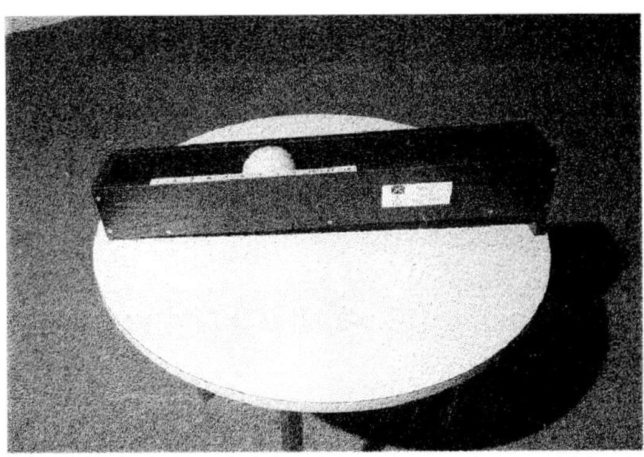

A ball stops at a typical position in the GOSSIP.

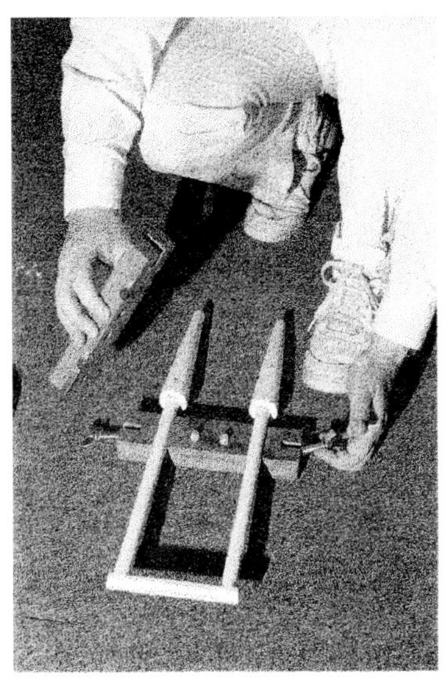

The author uses the WATCH to set a hoop